Realism and Reality

UNC | COLLEGE OF ARTS AND SCIENCES
Germanic and Slavic Languages and Literatures

From 1949 to 2004, UNC Press and the UNC Department of Germanic & Slavic Languages and Literatures published the UNC Studies in the Germanic Languages and Literatures series. Monographs, anthologies, and critical editions in the series covered an array of topics including medieval and modern literature, theater, linguistics, philology, onomastics, and the history of ideas. Through the generous support of the National Endowment for the Humanities and the Andrew W. Mellon Foundation, books in the series have been reissued in new paperback and open access digital editions. For a complete list of books visit www.uncpress.org.

Realism and Reality
Studies in the German Novelle of Poetic Realism

WALTER SILZ

UNC Studies in the Germanic Languages and Literatures
Number 11

Copyright © 1954

This work is licensed under a Creative Commons CC BY-NC-ND license. To view a copy of the license, visit http://creativecommons.org/licenses.

Suggested citation: Silz, Walter. *Realism and Reality: Studies in the German Novelle of Poetic Realism.* Chapel Hill: University of North Carolina Press, 1954. DOI: https://doi.org/10.5149/9781469658384_Silz

Library of Congress Cataloging-in-Publication Data
Names: Silz, Walter.
Title: Realism and reality : Studies in the German novelle of poetic realism / by Walter Silz.
Other titles: University of North Carolina Studies in the Germanic Languages and Literatures ; no. 11.
Description: Chapel Hill : University of North Carolina Press, [1954] Series: University of North Carolina Studies in the Germanic Languages and Literatures. | Includes bibliographical references.
Identifiers: LCCN 54011440 | ISBN 978-1-4696-5837-7 (pbk: alk. paper) | ISBN 978-1-4696-5838-4 (ebook)
Subjects: German fiction — 19th century — History and criticism. | Realism in literature.
Classification: LCC PD25 .N6 NO. 11

TO

P. K. S.

Table of Contents

		Page
Preface		xi
Chapter		
I.	Introduction: The Nature of the Novelle and of Poetic Realism	1
II.	Brentano, *Kasperl und Annerl*	17
III.	Arnim, *Der tolle Invalide*	29
IV.	Droste-Hülshoff, *Die Judenbuche*	36
V.	Stifter, *Abdias*	52
VI.	Grillparzer, *Der arme Spielmann*	67
VII.	Keller, *Romeo und Julia*	79
VIII.	Meyer, *Der Heilige*	94
IX.	Storm, *Der Schimmelreiter*	117
X.	Hauptmann, *Bahnwärter Thiel*	137
	Notes	155
	Index	167

PREFACE

The following group of studies is not in any wise intended as an "exhaustive" treatment of the German Novelle, or of the individual authors here represented. Nor does it attempt anything like a systematic account of Realism, or even a definition of it. My purpose has been simply to present analyses of certain Novellen that have impressed me as significant examples of Poetic Realism and of the art of Novelle-writing. I have accordingly limited myself to the period in which this style and this genre flowered simultaneously. This chronological delimitation has excluded both earlier important Novellen, notably Kleist's, and later ones. Even within the limits set, of course, no two writers would exactly agree in their choice of examples.

It might fairly be objected that a general *Zeitstil* needs to be studied in various forms of literature and indeed in various departments of cultural life. In reply, I should only say that the Novelle seems to me the most successful embodiment of the new realism, and in focusing a single beam of light on this one narrative type I have hoped to suggest the results of a wider but more diffuse illumination.

Considerable portions of the chapters on Droste-Hülshoff, Keller, and Storm have previously appeared in *The German Quarterly* and in the *Publications of the Modern Language Association of America*. The editors have kindly permitted me to reprint these passages. I am indebted to Professor Orie W. Long of Williams College for a helpful reading of my manuscript. Princeton University has generously subsidized the publication of this book through a grant from its Research Fund.

Walter Silz

Princeton University
Princeton, New Jersey
Summer 1953

CHAPTER ONE

INTRODUCTION: THE NATURE OF THE NOVELLE
AND OF POETIC REALISM

The German Novelle gets its name from the Italian *novella*, which in turn goes back to the Latin adjective *novus*. This form of narrative should then be essentially the account of a new, unheard-of happening, or at least a new, surprising treatment of matter already known. Its name, furthermore, attests its Romance provenience. Originally, like all story-telling, it stems from the Orient, but its European birthplace is the Renaissance, and its father is Boccaccio. The Renaissance placed a new high value on the individual; yet the "frame" in which Boccaccio's stories (like Scheherezade's *Arabian Nights*) are set indicates an over-individual background, the relation to a higher society. The Italian Renaissance produced, besides the *Decamerone*, a great store of *novellas*. Contemporaneous with Boccaccio's, or just slightly postdating his, are the "framed" stories of Chaucer's *Canterbury Tales*. Here, as in all these early *novellas*, a company (less often a single person) tell stories from their own experience, that is, they relate hitherto unknown matter, and the relating is oral and social. —It is characteristic of the later, German Novellen that, though the stories are sometimes in a "frame" or series, they are more often single stories, frequently in frames of their own.

In France, the *novella* developed with the tales of Margaret of Navarre in the 16th century, in Spain with those of Cervantes in the 16th and 17th. But Goethe and the Romanticists, who establish the genre in Germany both in theory and practice at the end of the 18th and beginning of the 19th century, go back essentially and consciously to Boccaccio. Goethe wrote the first true Novellen in Germany in his *Unterhaltungen deutscher Ausgewanderten* (1795), a sort of modern Decameron. Wieland had already earlier given a first definition, and subsequently produced examples, of the Novelle. But neither Wieland's shallow nor Goethe's traditional conception of the Novelle contained the seeds of new growth. Only in Heinrich von Kleist did Germany produce, in the Romantic period, a "Novellendichter" who was the peer of Boccaccio and Cervantes, and who inaugurated the particularly German evolution of this form. With the great impetus given by Kleist, the Novelle developed during the ensuing century more rapidly and more richly in Germany than in any other country. It has been said that the Novelle and the lyric constituted Germany's chief contribution to literature in the 19th century, paralleling the great novels of England, France, and Russia during that era.[1] With Kleist, the German Novelle "deepens its draft" and gains a capacity for dealing with major and tragic problems. It ceases to be a mere form of social entertainment and becomes a mature and high art, more concentrated and profound, a better mirror of the *Weltanschauung* of the age, than either the German drama or novel of the 19th century, taken as a whole, has been.

The Age of Goethe, the Classic-Romantic period, with its prodigious capacity for abstract thought, evolved an extensive literature of theory concerning the Novelle. Without attempting anything approaching a complete exposition of this literature and its continuation by later theorists, we may profitably take note of some of its salient points as criteria for our own examination of notable Novellen of the 19th century. As early as 1772, in the second edition of his *Don Sylvio von Rosalva* (I, 22), Wieland differentiated the Novelle from the "Roman" on the ground of the simplicity of its plot and its small size: the Novelle was simply a scaled-down novel, comparable to a playlet beside a full-sized play. Wieland's *Hexameron von Rosenhain* (1805) marks no advance, either in theory or practice, and Wieland is worth citing only to illustrate the absurd inadequacy of older theory to what the Novelle became in the hands of later and greater German writers.

Various passages of comment in the connective "frame" of Goethe's *Unterhaltungen*, taken together, constitute a "Novellentheorie" of a sort. Goethe does not, as a matter of fact, use the term "Novelle," but refers to the tales as "moralische Erzählungen,"—which two of them certainly are, the others being ghost-stories, anecdotes, and even a fanciful "Märchen." Goethe emphasizes the Boccaccian traits of novelty, appeal to a sophisticated upper class (gute Gesellschaft) and conformity to its standards of form and decorum, and social entertainment and diversion from a troublesome present. Thus, both in the types of narrative included and in the theoretical views expressed, Goethe's collection is a recapitulation of the past rather than a prophecy of the future of the German Novelle.

Years later, in an often-quoted conversation with Eckermann (January 29, 1827), Goethe delivered himself of a brief definition: "Was ist eine Novelle anders als eine sich ereignete, unerhörte Begebenheit?" This, again, though not without relevance later, primarily fits his own Novellen and represents the older, Boccaccian conception which in the 20th century Paul Ernst was to revive and exemplify. But neither Ernst nor other "purists" like Adolf von Grolman (who wrote the somewhat disgruntled article "Novelle" for the Merker-Stammler *Reallexikon*) do justice to the rich new flowering of this narrative form in the 19th century. The last of his own Novellen Goethe entitled simply *Novelle* (1827), as if to stress its exemplary character. Yet I venture to say that no one would ever have thought of calling this a Novelle had Goethe not so designated it. Here the Novelle is caught in the stagnant pool of allegory, while the live stream of development has taken a different course.

In a notable essay on Boccaccio (1801),[2] the young Friedrich Schlegel makes some significant remarks on the Novelle. He points out its supra-individual attitude as according with the rules and views of the high society which is its origin and home, and the anecdotal, as-yet-unknown character and particularity of its story. Its function as entertainment is still prominent; the "feine Gesellschaft" for which it is intended does not take the "was" (the matter) so strictly if only the "wie" (the manner) be engaging. The relation of all this to Goethe's *Unterhaltungen* is apparent. With characteristic paradox, however, Schlegel sees in the Novelle, because of its very objectivity, a vehicle for "indirect and concealed subjectivity" and for irony. August Wilhelm Schlegel, when he comes to speak of Boccaccio in his Berlin lectures of 1803-04, seems to echo some of his brother's views, and does not differentiate sharply between the Novelle and the novel.

Ludwig Tieck, who in his early years had written nondescript potboilers for Nicolai and then Novellen which are rather to be called gruesome "Märchen," like *Der blonde Eckbert* (1797), in his later, more realistic period contributed an important discussion[3] which emphasizes the need for a sharp focus and center. The Novelle, he says, puts into the strongest light a happening (Vorfall), great or small, which, though conceivable, is yet marvellous (wunderbar), perhaps unique.[4] He posits a turn (Wendung) in the story, a point at which it reverses itself, quite unexpectedly and yet naturally, that is, in keeping with character and circumstances, and develops consequences—so one might render Tieck's slightly curious wording—inherent in the premises but not hitherto manifest. The Novelle, Tieck continues, admits of all colors and characters, but will in every case have this striking turning-point (jenen auffallenden Wendepunkt) which distinguishes it from all other types of narration. He also ascribes to it objectivity, that is, impartiality and moral indifference. This brief discussion is fruitful both in the precision of its chief criterion and in the latitude it otherwise accords the Novelle.

There is a certain affinity between Tieck's evaluation and the much more publicized one of Paul Heyse forty years later. Both Heyse's theory and his production were more extensive than Tieck's. Heyse wrote over one hundred Novellen, few of which are read today. He also edited, with Hermann Kurz, a collection of Novellen. In the Introduction to the first edition of this *Deutscher Novellenschatz*,[5] and again thirty years later in his *Jugenderinnerungen und Bekenntnisse*,[6] Heyse summed up his views, which culminate in the celebrated "Falkentheorie." The Novelle, he says, deals with significant human fate or conflict, revealing to us by means of an unusual happening a new aspect of human nature. It presents a specific case, sharply outlined within a restricted framework, just as the chemist must isolate the interaction of certain elements in his experiment to illustrate some law of Nature.[7] The novel has a wider horizon and more manifold problems; it embraces various concentric "Lebenskreise." The Novelle restricts itself to one circle and one conflict: "in einem *einzigen* Kreise einen *einzelnen* Konflikt," and it can suggest only in "abbreviation" the relation of its persons to the general life (xviii). It has a definite individual character or "profile:" "etwas Eigenartiges, Spezifisches schon in der blossen Anlage ... eine starke, deutliche *Silhouette*," and it can be summarized in a few lines, as are the tales in Boccaccio's *Decamerone* (xix). From the story of the falcon in this work (the 9th story of the 5th day) Heyse derives his desideratum of the "Falke," that is, the specific thing that differentiates a particular Novelle from a thousand others.

Heyse's theory had considerable vogue for a time, but of late years it has been much criticised. Heyse discerned correctly the tendency of the Novelle toward delimitation and isolation and its concentration on one central conflict. It is true also that the story can usually be summed up in brief and striking, often paradoxical, formulation. But any great work of literature is likely to have a markedly individual "silhouette" which renders it unmistakable among its kind, and in making a sort of requirement of the "falcon"[8] Heyse has stressed a feature of external form rather than internal organization.

Heyse's friend, Theodor Storm, himself a prolific "Novellist," took no stock in the falcon-theory. Already in his period of "lyrical" Novellen, Storm had recognized "Beschränkung und Isolierung" as the essence of the Novelle (letter to Brinkmann, November 22, 1851). Thirty years later, when his experience and art had deepened, he expressed with some ardor and pride his conviction that the Novelle had become a major form of literature: "Sie ist nicht mehr, wie einst, die kurzgehaltene Darstellung einer durch ihre Ungewöhnlichkeit fesselnden und einen überraschenden Wendepunkt darbietenden Begebenheit [a sort of summary of Goethe and Tieck]; die heutige Novelle ist die Schwester des Dramas und die strengste Form der Prosadichtung. Gleich dem Drama behandelt sie die tiefsten Probleme des Menschenlebens; gleich diesem verlangt sie zu ihrer Vollendung einen im Mittelpunkte stehenden Konflikt, von welchem aus das Ganze sich organisiert, und demzufolge die geschlossenste Form und die Ausscheidung alles Unwesentlichen; sie duldet nicht nur, sie stellt auch die höchsten Forderungen der Kunst."[9]

Several years after this, Friedrich Spielhagen, who was primarily a writer of problem-novels, added a new point to the theory of the Novelle and of its relation to the novel.[10] The latter, he said, deals with characters still developing and being determined by their "Umwelt" or *milieu*, whereas the Novelle deals, in a brief action, with characters, few in number, who are already fully developed (fertig) and who, being brought into a crucial conflict, merely reveal or unfold their inherent natures. In the older Novelle, the particular concatenation of circumstances preponderated in determining the outcome, in the modern Novelle the peculiar nature of the engaged characters does so. The procedure of the Novelle is one of multiplication: with few factors a definite product is quickly calculated. The procedure of the novel is one of addition of a long series of various terms. Hence, both in ultimate aim and in artistic economy, the Novelle is decidedly like the drama, whereas the novel, being the complete antipode of the drama, is by the same token fundamentally different from the Novelle.

A recent writer on the Novelle, Johannes Klein,[11] sees three chief features as characteristic of it: 1) a central event (defined by Goethe as an "unerhörte Begebenheit," by others in other terms); 2) a "Leitmotiv" (which may be a symbolic object like Heyse's falcon or the two black horses in Kleist's *Kohlhaas*) together with subordinate motifs; 3) an "Idee" (according to Heyse expressible in a sentence) which deepens and unifies the story. In the novel, Klein points out, character develops; in the Novelle it is merely tested by event. The novel operates with what a man is; the Novelle, with what happens to him. The novel unites several actions, the Novelle is organized around one action. The novel mirrors the world in individual destinies; the Novelle reflects in an individual destiny a segment of the world. The novel seeks the law; the Novelle loves chance. The novel answers Fate's question to man through his life and development; the Novelle likes to leave the question open.

Already in the middle of the 19th century the then dominant aesthetician, Friedrich Theodor Vischer, had somewhat similarly discriminated these two forms of prose narration. The Novelle is to the novel, said Vischer, as a single beam is to a great flood of light: "Die Novelle verhält sich zum Roman wie ein Strahl zu einer Lichtmasse." The Novelle gives, not the comprehensive view of world-conditions, but a segment (Ausschnitt) of them which with momentary intensity opens up a perspective upon the greater whole; it gives, not the complete development of a personality, but a piece of human life which contains a tension, a crisis, and through a turning-point in character and fate demonstrates with sharp accent what human life in general is.[12]

That the distinction between the Novelle and the novel is not simply one of length but of inner organization has been pretty generally recognized. The Novelle cannot be panoramic and leisurely; it must be concentrated and intensified, limited to one central conflict of crucial importance. Heyse had demanded this "einzelner Konflikt;" Storm reiterated it when he wrote to Erich Schmidt (October 9, 1879) that, in contrast to the novel, the Novelle calls for a stricter, more compact form and a conflict around which the whole is organized.

Time has a different value in the two narrative forms. The novel has more time at its disposal, and it tells its story in "historical," chronological order, at an unhurried pace. The Novelle, on the contrary, has an accelerated, sometimes a feverish pace: it hastens toward a climax, it tends to be all climax, without the before and after of the novel. Instead of unrolling past, present, and future in sequence, it seizes upon a fateful moment of dramatic presentness from which the past and the future are illuminated in a flash—"ein Menschenleben durch die unendlich sinnliche Kraft einer Schicksalsstunde ausgedrückt."[13] The Novelle often inverts the chronological order, starting with the conclusion and then going back or part-way back to show how this final situation came to be. As to subject-matter, the novel prefers the typical and social, the Novelle the singular and isolated.

The anecdote, like the Novelle, spotlights one single event, but so much so that it usually amounts only to a "pointe" of limited and momentary effect. It is apt to share with the German "short story" the purpose of transitory entertainment without higher artistic pretensions; and both are often used as journalistic space-fillers.[14] The anecdote, as Vischer pointed out, is usually comical, whereas the Novelle moves also in the realm of tragedy, in fact more frequently than the novel does.[15] The anecdote can add a characterizing touch to an already known personality, but it cannot produce a personality, as the Novelle can. There is an undeniable kinship, however, between the Novelle and the anecdote, closer than that between the Novelle and the novel. Some of the tales in the *Decamerone* are really anecdotes, and so is at least one in Goethe's *Unterhaltungen;* Kleist, a master of the Novelle, is also a master of the anecdote. By its very etymology (Greek *anekdotos* = unpublished) the anecdote shares with the Novelle that element of "the unheard-of that has actually happened" which Goethe's later definition emphasized.

The Novelle shows a subtle kinship with the ballad. Both have the quality of dramatic tension and concentration on a central event; both deal with an unusual, even baffling, individual case in which a general law or truth is manifested. In both, the author maintains an objective attitude. One might say that the Novelle is to the "Roman" approximately as the "Ballade" is to the "Epos." Novelle and ballad both tend to a laconic, allusive style, which leaves much unsaid between the lines and demands imaginative cooperation of the reader. Both resort to symbolism to imply what they have not space to say. Both, so to speak, give a series of luminous points on a dark background and thereby suggest a continuous line. It is significant that Brentano's *Kasperl und Annerl* and several of Storm's later Novellen are based on ballads.

The relatedness of Novelle and drama was recognized already by the Romanticists. The greatest dramatist of that period, Kleist, was also its greatest "Novellendichter." Shakespeare, of course, drew some of his plays from *novellas*, and Otto Ludwig, for example, could adhere very closely to Hoffmann's plot in his dramatization of *Das Fräulein von Scuderi*. The objective impersonality in the attitude of the author toward his characters; the central crisis to which the action rises and from which it falls, the peripeteia or "Wendepunkt;" the concentration on an isolated, enhanced world, an actual or figurative "stage" (to the delimitation of which the frequent "framing" of the Novelle contributes); the sense of urgency and propulsive "drive" in contrast to the slower epic pace of the novel; the throwing of light on only the "engaged" sides of the actors and yet suggesting the complete "round" of their personalities—all these traits the Novelle at its best shares with the drama. In the hands of the older Romance masters the *novella* maintained a basically epic "Einstellung;" in the hands of the great German "Novellisten" of the 19th century the Novelle takes on, more or less consciously, a dramatic aspect. Storm considered it a surrogate for the drama in a period when the latter had relinquished its primacy.[16] Keller's dearest ambition was to be a dramatist. Meyer conceived his greatest Novellen first as plays. And at the end of the century we see, as at its beginning—in Hauptmann as in Kleist—a dramatist making his mark as a "Novellist." It is very likely—though it would be difficult to prove in detail—that the German drama and Novelle influenced each other considerably in their development during the 19th century.

This is, at any rate, another indication of the enlargement of the Novelle in Germany in this period. The original Romance form, as exemplified still in Goethe's *Unterhaltungen*, with their emphasis on piquant event and piquant narration within the bounds of upper-class decorum, no longer sufficed the new century. A characteristically German emphasis on ethical and philosophical "Bedeutung" operated to burst the bonds of traditional form and raise the Novelle to a primary type of literature, a receptacle for themes as momentous as those of novel or drama. "Alles," we read in the Introduction to the Heyse-Kurz *Novellenschatz* (I, xiv), "alles, was eine Menschenbrust bewegt, gehört in [ihren] Kreis.... Von dem einfachen Bericht eines merkwürdigen Ereignisses oder einer sinnreich erfundenen abenteuerlichen Geschichte hat sich die Novelle nach und nach zu der Form entwickelt, in welcher gerade die tiefsten und wichtigsten sittlichen Fragen zur Sprache kommen." One could, after a moment's consideration, draw up an impressive list of vital "Lebensfragen" treated in German Novellen; some of these we shall encounter in our subsequent studies.[17]

In view of all the affinities and enlargements of the Novelle which we have thus surveyed, is it still possible to "define" it as a form of literature? On closer examination, not one of the traditional criteria evolved by successive theorists appears strictly indispensable. A Novelle does not *have* to have a "falcon;" only a few of Boccaccio's do, and not very many such central symbols occur in German Novellen by actual count. On the other hand, a novel may have one; the talisman in Scott's novel of that name functions in general like the amulet in Meyer's Novelle. The "Wendepunkt," likewise, though it is often present, more or less midway in the story, is not an exclusive prerogative of the Novelle; novels and plays also have a critical turning-point, a peripeteia, in the hero's fortunes; only in the Novelle, because of its briefer measure and its restriction to one "zentrales Ereignis," this feature stands out more starkly. Leitmotifs, too, are not limited to the Novelle; they occur in novels such as Mann's *Buddenbrooks*. The "frame," though often an aid to the objectivation, isolation, and distancing characteristic of the Novelle, is not invariably found. Many Novellen do present a "fertiger Charakter" in the hero, who is tested, not molded, by the central event. But this is not a *sine qua non:* we shall see in several distinguished examples later the compassing of a whole lifetime. A small number of persons is involved in the focal action, to be sure, but it is left to the skill of the author to sketch in a number of more remote figures, and suggest a complete social "Umwelt."

In *Der arme Heinrich* by Hartmann von Aue, a brief epic composed about 1200 in an age of long verse-romances, we have, in the midst of these medieval "novels," a sort of Novelle. Had Hartmann been writing in the 19th century, he doubtless would have told his tale in prose, instead of the dominant Middle High German rimed couplets. His little story fulfills a surprising number of the criteria of the Novelle which we have noted. The fact that we have here virtually a Novelle, long before the name or theory of such a genre were thought of, suggests that the Novelle represents something like a "natural" form in literature:[18] a narrative of limited size and scope, which because of its nature tends to employ some or all of the devices hitherto considered that make for compactness and maximum expressiveness. Hence these features, though not individually indispensable, yet all have a certain validity as partial and approximate descriptions of a highly concentrated, highly artistic form of narrative literature. To the Germans, who tend all too readily to diffuse and formless novels, and who do not take naturally to the witty acuity of the anecdote or the slightness and pungency of the short-story, the Novelle has offered a salutary challenge to delimit, to compass infinite riches in a little room, to emulate Goethe's dictum "In der Beschränkung zeigt sich erst der Meister."

The matter of the Novelle, with its bias toward particular cases of human experience, tends toward realism; at the same time its form, as we have seen, calls for a high degree of conscious art. This combination is precisely the ideal of the so-called Poetic Realism, and this, I believe, is the reason why the finest flowering of the Novelle coincides with the period of that literary movement. Its name is awkward and unsatisfactory, like most literary labels, and its dates not precisely definable. It emerges gradually from Romanticism in the 1830's or somewhat earlier, and is succeeded, with a more marked boundary, by Naturalism in the late 1880's; but all such date-lines in literature are approximate and subject to overlapping. It manifests itself, like any *Zeitstil*, in various forms of literature, but in the narrative, and above all in the Novelle, it may claim to be the particular contribution of the 19th century to German literary style.

The "Goethe-Zeit," the Classic-Romantic era of about 1770 to 1830, was the age of Idealism; its intellectual background was formed by the uninterrupted growth of German idealistic philosophy from Kant to Schelling. Broadly speaking, Classicism tended toward the idealized, generalized, and typical; Romanticism toward the unique, imaginary, and supernatural. Both departed, in different directions, from reality; both might be called subjective in their attitude toward the world of things.

But this world of things was changing. The Paris revolution of 1830 had economic and social repercussions in Germany, and gave a great impetus to political Liberalism, the rise and flourishing of which substantially coincides with the period we are discussing. The immediate literary outgrowth of the revolution, Young Germany, had no poetic value, yet it helped to bring literature closer to the issues of the day. The first German railroad began operating in 1835. Industrialization was beginning, if as yet on a modest scale. Newspapers and magazines were becoming a force, and incidentally exerting a pervasive influence in favor of prose. The exact sciences were advancing apace, after the stimulus given by Romantic theorists. In reaction from the idealistic-transcendental religiosity of the Romantic era, a sceptical, iconoclastic, "diesseitig" spirit was being applied to religion by such men as David Friedrich Strauss and Ludwig Feuerbach. Historiography, to which, again, Romanticism had given a mighty impetus, was developing more factual methods and emphasizing the study of primary sources. A wave of pessimism, induced by the experiencing of history as fate during the Napoleonic years and by disillusionment following the imposition of governmental repression after 1815, was reinforced by a second wave of disappointment over the unsuccessful revolutions of 1848; and into this favorable atmosphere the sobering philosophy of Schopenhauer began, about the middle of the century, to infuse its delayed effects.

Under the stress of these altered conditions, writers developed the element of realism which was already present in Romanticism. No hard and fast line can be drawn here, for later Romanticists like Brentano and Arnim, as we shall see, and Tieck (after about 1822) show marked realistic traits—to say nothing of Kleist, who in such a figure as the knacker of Döbbeln in *Kohlhaas* anticipates Naturalism by eighty years.

As Herford has pointed out,[19] the Romantic "return to Nature" had been by no means a mere escape, but the source of a new power of seeing the world about us as it really is. The Poetic Realists, then, could preserve a good deal of Romanticism, even as they sharpened and sobered its perception of things in keeping with the new insights of an age that felt realities pressing more insistently upon it. They kept much of the Romantic "Phantasie" and "Stimmungskunst," and even of the poetic interpretation of life. For it must be remembered that the early Poetic Realists still stood in the shadow of the great "Goethe-Zeit" and had themselves grown up in the tradition of idealistic philosophy.

What naturally resulted, therefore, was a compromise between pure "Romantik" at the one extreme and "Naturalismus" at the other, between the poetisation of the world and the stark reflection of things as things, without symbolical valuation or interpretation. This compromise was called Poetic Realism. The term was coined by Otto Ludwig, and he was the most consistent, though not the earliest, exponent of it in theory and practice.[20] The realist, as Ludwig conceives him—in contrast to the idealist, whom he never wearies of disparaging, especially in the person of Schiller, as a falsifier of reality—the Poetic Realist gives us reality unmixed with his private feelings and reflections, "gibt die Sache selbst unvermischt mit seinem Ich."[21] "Man schildere die Welt, wie sie ist," is Ludwig's directive; or, to use a homely kitchen figure, one must serve up life as it is, in its own juice: "Wir müssen die Sache selbst und in ihrer eignen Sauce geben."[22]

It is not just a matter of "imitating" actuality, however; the poet's artistic intelligence is a factor in the process. He strives to give his picture unity, selecting essentials (das Wichtige) and discarding non-essentials (Unwesentliches); his result is not raw Nature, but an artistic reflection of it: "nicht die gemeine Natur, sondern ein künstlerisches Spiegelbild derselben" (*Schriften*, VI, 10). Realism selects and poeticizes, like the memory: "Die Poesie verfährt nach den Gesetzen der Erinnerung: sie ändert nicht, was geschehen, aber sie mildert es künstlerisch" (VI, 42). It aims at artistic reproduction of reality, avoiding any illusion of vulgar factuality.[23]

True poetry, Ludwig maintains, seeks everywhere the inner

law of things that lies behind their fortuitous appearances: "Die wahre Poesie muss sich ganz von der äusseren Gegenwart loslösen, sozusagen von der wirklichen Wirklichkeit. Sie darf bloss das festhalten, was dem Menschen zu allen Zeiten eignet, seine wesentliche Natur, und muss dies in individuelle Gestalten kleiden, d.h. sie muss realistische Ideale schaffen" (V, 411). It is interesting to observe how much there still is of the older idealism in Ludwig's position; one might describe this as Realistic Idealism and detect in it an echo of Schiller's discrimination of "real" and "true" Nature in his famous essay *On Naïve and Reflective Poetry*.[24] Ludwig takes a middle ground. The world of Poetic Realism "stands midway between the objective truth of things and the law which our mind is impelled to read into them" (V, 459). The Naturalist is intent on the breadth and multiplicity of things, the Idealist on an abstract unity; each of these directions is one-sided; Poetic Realism unites them in a "künstlerische Mitte" (*ibid.*).

The estimation of "reality" is of course subject to historical shifts. Naturalism, at the end of the 19th century, professed to report reality as it was, especially its seamy side. Classicism, a century earlier, had subordinated reality to ideas. In our own mid-20th century, in turn, much of reality has become unreal, or suspect as a mere projection of the consciousness. In Kafka's world, now so much in vogue, reality has certainly lost all "realness." On the other hand, what gives to the epoch of Poetic Realism its unique and irretrievable charm is its productive reconciliation of a heightened sense of real things with a conviction of their imaginative, spiritual meaning.

The Poetic Realists saw the world more sharply than anyone had done before them. Careful observation and recording of the concrete details that make up *milieu* is their forte. But they subordinated these things to an artistic purpose and plan; they filtered them, as it were, through a poetic medium which transformed crude fact into artistic truth. They did not believe in photographic reproduction, but reserved the right of selection and stylization. They steered a course between what Ludwig termed "the subjective ardors of lyrical rhetoric" and the "thin, aimless speech of vulgar reality" (V, 264). In earlier attempts to write dialogue, Ludwig once confessed to Auerbach, he had lapsed into naturalism, attempting to reproduce the speech of actual life; but he found this "over-great immediacy" inartistic, and abandoned it.[25] A similar self-reproach is recorded of Gottfried Keller. He was unhappy over his last novel, *Martin Salander* (1886), in which, contrary to his wont, he had adhered closely to actuality. He protested to a friend: "Es ist nicht schön! Es ist nicht schön! Es ist zu wenig Poesie darin!" Beguiled by the incipient Naturalism of the time, he had betrayed, he felt, his lifelong principle "wahr und schön."[26]

Ludwig's play *Der Erbförster* is full of real-life persons smoking, dancing, eating, playing cards, and quarrelling; they speak a natural, colloquial language, but it is somewhat "raised:" no dialect occurs, no vulgarisms, no criminal *argot*—though two of the characters are criminal revolutionists. The poetic "Stimmung" of the forest is preserved throughout. "Der grüne rauschende Wald," the author specified, "muss dem Stück stets über die Schulter sehen;" it was to represent "schöne (nicht zu enggenommene) Wirklichkeit."[27] The last phrase is something like a definition of Poetic Realism—the reality of Naturalism, certainly, is not "schön" and is "zu enggenommen"—and the first phrase, in thought and expression, is proof of the residual Romanticism in this new Realism.[28]

Man is here still rooted in Nature, his character and life are deeply affected by it. The Forester himself is a king in his domain and an idealist in his calling, not yet an employee or a factory worker. Similarly, Hebbel's Meister Anton in *Maria Magdalene* is still a rugged personality, a sceptical idealist, capable of the heroic in speech and action—a contrast to the carpenter in Ibsen's *Ghosts,* who is a real "little man" of the proletariat, speaking and acting unheroically. The poetic and idealistic conception of "Beruf" or calling is characteristic of Poetic Realism: the slater in Ludwig's *Zwischen Himmel und Erde*, the soldier in Brentano's *Kasperl und Annerl* and Arnim's *Invalide*, the forester in *Der Erbförster*, the dikebuilder in Storm's *Schimmelreiter* are semi-artists who identify themselves with their craft and express themselves through it. There is also a close connection with the regional literature or "Heimatdichtung" that was one of the most fruitful tendencies of this period, quite different from the cosmopolitanism of the "Goethe-Zeit." Poetic Realism tends to have the coloring of a particular region and landscape to which its persons are attached. It tends toward provincialism rather than nationalism. It deals by preference with the "Kleinstadt" or "Dorf," whereas Naturalism was to turn to the metropolis and its masses. The social matrix of Poetic Realism is the liberalized middle-class, the "Bürgertum."

While Naturalism professes to take things at their face value, Poetic Realism has a strong leaning toward symbolism, for it believes that things have deeper meanings than appear on their surfaces. Wilhelm Raabe, one of the great narrators of this time, said that all genuine poetry must needs be symbolical.[29] By selecting from among the raw materials of experience the significant things, Poetic Realism invested them with a higher reality, indeed, as Ludwig thought, achieved something more real than reality, for it caught the essence underlying accidental appearances. Art, he insisted, should not be impoverished but enriched reality (V, 265). Mere reality, he would have agreed with Paul Ernst, is devoid of talent.[30] The here and now which Naturalism seeks to convey is, paradoxically speaking, nowhere; the chance fact is often furthest from the truth; the poet's reality shows clearly the heart of things, while the inchoate chaff of "actual" realities obscures it. Vrenchen in *Romeo und Julia* is more real than any of the Swiss country girls of her time out of whose traits Keller's poetic alchemy created a new and immortal being.

All literature is realistic, in the sense that it tries to discern and depict the real truth of life. But different ages, and their poets, have differed as to what they considered the "real things" to be. To some ages, gods are real, peopling heaven and earth; to others, ideas and ideals alone seem real; to still others, physical or chemical actions of matter upon matter constitute the reality of existence, and man's imaginings about gods, or beauty, or things spiritual are but luxuries or self-deceptions. Such an age we seem to be living in today. But there has probably never been a completely materialistic age, nor a purely idealistic one, since human history began; and our own time, with its awfully augmented powers of physical destruction, provides, in its application of those powers, a striking vindication of the might of ideas, not to say myths.

What makes Poetic Realism in Germany so significant is that here, in an age still ringing with the idealism of the Classic-Romantic culture, and yet already flooded with increasing evidence of "emancipated" Man's dominion over Nature, a compromise was found between the "ideal" and the "real"—not simply for lack of a more original solution, but out of a conviction that this is *the* solution, the truth of life. The 19th century, wide-eyed before a rapidly expanding world of real things, was ready to concede greater importance to "das Gemeine," over which Schiller's sublime spirit had soared as over "wesenlosem Scheine;" and yet this century cherished the inherited conviction of the primacy of ideas. A theme we shall find running through many of the Novellen of the century is that of the struggle to keep the inner citadel of the personality inviolate from the world—a problem that, needless to say, is still with us in the 20th century. Michael Kohlhaas, after his major decision to dedicate himself to an ideal, rejoicing to feel his own soul "in order" amid a disordered world; Friedrich Mergel, imprisoned and doomed by his entirely private sense of guilt; the Poor Fiddler, dividing off by his symbolical chalk-line the world of sordid necessities in which he earns his paltry bread from the essential world of his art and his dreams; Apollonius Nettenmaier, mutilating his outer life for the sake of preserving the inner from the defilement of guilt and sex; Thiel, the crossing-tender, in his groping mysticism struggling to sequester his higher life from his sensual everyday existence—all these men in their living and dying are determined by ideas, not by the "compelling facts" of the outside world. And so the Novellen we are about to consider demonstrate, each in its own way, both literature's increased awareness of the realities of life and the fact that the only real realities are the persuasions of the human mind.

CHAPTER TWO

BRENTANO, *GESCHICHTE VOM BRAVEN KASPERL UND DEM SCHÖNEN ANNERL* (1817)[1]

Clemens Brentano is one of the greatest lyrical geniuses of Germany, a poet of eminently musical temper and deep, often mystical feeling. He is also one of the most gifted of German story-tellers, endlessly inventive, a born "spinner of yarns." Both as poet and as narrator, he displays a rich but wayward imagination, and his work is uneven in quality. His private life was one of the most tragic and torn in the history of literature, and is marked by the unending quest for religious peace and stability of mind. The most fruitful interest of his early years was that in the "Volkslieder;" the monumental collection of these he made with Achim von Arnim, *Des Knaben Wunderhorn*, left its mark on German lyric poetry all through the 19th century.

If this be, in briefest outline, the literary physiognomy of Brentano, then his *Geschichte vom braven Kasperl und dem schönen Annerl* reflects it faithfully, and the Novelle-form proves in this instance, among other things, its capacity for conveying the character of its author. The facts about the story's sources and its genesis are not yet wholly clarified, but that it is intimately connected with the folk-ballad, particularly with one in the *Wunderhorn* entitled "Weltlich Recht," and probably with old chronicles, of which Brentano was an avid reader (among them the memoirs of a 16th-century executioner), has been established beyond doubt.

The story exhibits all the chief features which theorists of the Novelle, before and since its time, have set forth as characteristic of this genre: it deals with a single central conflict that affects the lives of a few mature individuals; it has the "Wendepunkt" which Tieck demanded (the hero's denunciation of his father and brother, exactly midway in the account) and the "Falke" of Heyse's theory (at least one may see something like this in Kasper's tinsel wreath); it has "Leitmotive" aplenty; its dominant "Idee" could be summarized briefly— and paradoxically— as too much of honor, or culpable excess in a virtue. It has an elaborate and skilfully manipulated "frame," in this case with two narrators and two "depths" of view. One could classify it as a "Problem-Novelle" in so far as it debates an ethical problem, the deep and complicated one of Honor; and it does this not merely in speeches, as do the later "Diskussionsnovellen" of Tieck, but by means of characters and action. One could call it the first German "Dorf- und Bauernnovelle," in so far as it is the earliest Novelle to deal with the peasant folk and with the tragedy of humble lives—a new direction in which later on Immermann and Droste-Hülshoff and Grillparzer were to follow.

Concern with the common folk is by no means unknown to German Romanticism; in fact it can be found all through the "Deutsche Bewegung" which comprises the "Sturm und Drang" (or Pre-Romanticism) and Romanticism proper. This whole period admired the "unverdorbenes Volk" both because these represented the traditional and the past which had such high value for the historically-minded Romanticists (and Pre-Romanticists) and also because such naïve folk embody a simplicity and wholeness which the complicated cultured person longs to regain —and here, in particular, an unshakeable religious calm such as Brentano pursued all his life in vain.[2] If the ancient peasant woman of this story has elder sisters in the "Bäuerinnen" from whose wrinkled lips the Grimm brothers took down their "Volksmärchen," she has a younger sister in Chamisso's "alte Waschfrau." Heine was akin to Brentano in this trait also, that at times, as in the *Harzreise*, he evinced a genuine respect and understanding for the common folk who were poles apart from his own complex and sophisticated mentality. An interesting detail in Brentano's story, as in Eichendorff's *Taugenichts*, is the suggestion of the actual gathering of folksongs from the mouths of the rustic "Volk"—another "Romantic" activity that had realistic implications.

While this concern with villagers and peasants makes for a marvellous realism in Brentano's tale, there are other elements in it that hark back to the Romantic in the sense of the fantastic and unreal. It is in fact a Brentanian blend of Romanticism, Realism, myth, and "Märchen," with a touch of religious allegory. The over-great wealth of motifs testifies to the fecundity of Brentano's imagination, but detracts from that "Schlankheit" or slenderness which characterizes the Novelle at its best. To be sure, even Kleist's *Kohlhaas* entered, at its end, the twilight zone of supernaturalism; but Brentano's story is far more extensively overrun with the lianas of fairy-tale, fate-tragedy, and superstition, all of them growing out of the dark soil of Romantic addiction to the "night-side of Nature."

Thus the purely human tragedy of Annerl is impaired by making her subject to a fatal predestination. When we first see her, a child of three years, she is already marked for wrongdoing and death on the block, as is evidenced by the rattling of the executioner's sword at her approach and soon afterwards by the gruesome omen of the criminal's severed head rolling over and biting her dress. Logically—within the illogic of fatalism—we should have to suppose that the executioner's attempt to "break" her fate by scratching the child's neck with his blade would not have availed, or that it was part of fate that he should be stayed in this attempt. The belief in such a "Schwertaberglaube" of course is, or was, characteristic of the "Volk," and to this extent its use here is not unrealistic.[3] Annerl's motivation is further obfuscated by magic, for her seducer at the last confesses having used "certain medicines of magical potency" to assail her virtue—surely a gratuitous touch! A last-minute reprieve for Annerl is prevented by the double accident that the messenger's horse collapses and artillery maneuvers in the vicinity drown out his voice. Such contrivances and arabesques of Brentano's irrepressible fancy add to the mystery and picturesqueness of his tale, but lessen its realistic and tragic force.

An astounding wealth of motifs is compressed into this little story of not much more than thirty printed pages. What one might call the core narrative is a true Novelle, admirably compact, as though Brentano had taken lessons in cogent realism and dramatic objectivity from Heinrich von Kleist, his associate in Berlin a few years earlier and the stern editorial abridger of Brentano's contributions to the *Berliner Abendblätter*. Brentano gets under way briskly: in two brief paragraphs he has created mood and suspense, introduced his outer and inner narrators, and made the latter immediately impressive. Then in the third paragraph a dramatic little street scene ensues, spiced with a certain irony on "public opinion." Then the crowd disperses, and we are left alone in the stillness of early morning with the two persons who will tell us the story.

The central action of this story is conveyed through a series of admirably terse, dramatic, vividly real scenes: the attack on the mill, Kasper's discovery of his own father and brother as the armed robbers, Kasper's suicide; the scene in the palace courtyard, where the narrator struggles to gain admittance to the Duke, the wild ride to the place of execution, the arrival there and the ensuing disclosures, to the point (short of the final moralization) where the old woman, like a personification of Charity and Fate, performs her last attentions to Annerl's body —this sequence could hardly be improved on for rapid and compelling narration.

A premonitory dream creates mood and foreshadows the action to come (104);[4] ominous hints of some awful tragedy as yet hidden are thrown out: "Ich ahnte, ein schweres Leid müsse auf ihr lasten" (101). Little by little, not forthrightly but by allusion, adumbration, retrogression, the lugubrious past and the lowering future are revealed. This gradual and interrupted unrolling of a dreadful tale by a norn-like old woman who is involved in these events and yet, like an antique Chorus, apart from them and a commentator on them, is the greatest achievement of Brentano's narrative art. His procedure is like that of the "analytical exposition" in the drama: he starts his action just before the final catastrophe, concentrating it all in a few hours preceding an impending execution. This gives a prodigious sense of urgency and dramatic tension. Step by step the past is brought to view through "Rückgriffe" from the "frame," while at the same time the present action, punctuated by the striking of the hours, advances inexorably. This "depth" procedure—not unlike that recently employed by Thomas Mann in *Doktor Faustus*—in addition makes possible an unusual amount of tragic irony, where a character says more than he realizes, or we know more than he does of what hangs over him.

This Novelle has a double "frame," with two narrators, the author and the old woman, both of whom are implicated in the current action, and two perspectives of narration. We are thus twice removed from the gruesomeness of the actual occurrences —and Brentano is at times unnecessarily gruesome.[5] The "frame" interrupts the story at times, to avoid its becoming monotonous and to divide it into sections—for example, at the point, just past the middle, where the old woman, having completed the story of Kasper, starts out to walk with the narrator to the place of execution and to tell him the story of Annerl on the way (109).

The narrator of the outer frame makes no pretense of complete objectivity; he frequently betrays his own emotion as he is progressively touched, shaken, and completely crushed (gerührt, erschüttert, ganz zermalmt) by what he hears. He is deeply moved by the old woman's simple faith and repose, which contrast with his own religious doubts and soul-searchings (that are of course Brentano's): will all my efforts and questings ever bring me to the calm trust in which this pious soul spends the night on a doorstep, sure of the morning and the Friend who will come with it? Shall I attain that City and that Friend, or perish, weary, before the gate? This passage (93) is a religious poem in prose, and it parallels some of Brentano's verse ones of these critical years.

Then the narrator muses upon the deep and still unsolved problem of Honor (98). And perhaps most interesting of all is his digression on being a "Schriftsteller" or writer, the disinclination of the German (versus the Frenchman) to admit himself one, and the uneasy feeling that to make a profession of writing is to throw one's humanity out of healthy balance: "Es ist auch wirklich ein verdächtiges Ding um einen Dichter von Profession, der es nicht nur nebenher ist. Man kann sehr leicht zu ihm sagen: 'Mein Herr, ein jeder Mensch hat, wie Hirn, Herz, Magen, Milz, Leber und dergleichen, auch eine Poesie im Leibe; wer aber eines dieser Glieder überfüttert, verfüttert oder mästet und es über alle andre hinübertreibt, ja es gar zum Erwerbzweige macht, der muss sich schämen vor seinem ganzen übrigen Menschen. Einer, der von der Poesie lebt, hat das Gleichgewicht verloren, und eine übergrosse Gänseleber, sie mag noch so gut schmecken, setzt doch immer eine kranke Gans voraus.' Alle Menschen, welche ihr Brot nicht im Schweiss ihres Angesichts verdienen, müssen sich einigermassen schämen; und das fühlt einer, der noch nicht ganz in der Tinte war, wenn er sagen soll, er sei ein Schriftsteller" (99). Here we have, already clearly anticipated, Thomas Mann's self-irony and chronic "bad conscience" about his art, perhaps most openly avowed in the famous fourth chapter of *Tonio Kröger*.

Brentano's story is an excellent illustration of how decisive the choice of a narrator, or an "inner" narrator, can be for the style and character of a Novelle. Told directly by an omniscient and invisible author, this tale would not have the immediacy, the color, the woodcut-like angularity and starkness, the suspense and impact which it gets by being channelled through this stoical, rustic, somewhat helpless and slightly confused old woman. It would be something like Coleridge's immortal Rime *not* told by the ancient mariner.

The stylization in terms of the inner narrator is not, however, carried through without some inconsistencies. Occasionally the omniscient author infringes on his appointed spokesman. Since, for example, Kasper told his grandmother of the attack on the mill only "in great haste" at her window (106), she could not well have known all the details she recounted on the preceding pages. Moreover, the style of narration imputed to her in this account does not accord with her character but is Brentano's own splendidly vivid and dramatic style. Also, she knows in complete detail all that happened further (107f.), although Kasper did not return to report to her before his death, and she had secluded herself from everyone else (108).

But these are minor lapses, which only a critical reader would detect. More serious, it seems to me, is the overshadowing of the true folk-world, which old Anna Margaret represents, by the world of the aristocrats and their illicit amours. The weakling Count Grossinger, his shadowy sister, and the conventional Duke —an echo of the *Märchen*-figure of the good King who intervenes to make all things right[6] —these are thrust so far into the foreground at the end as to make us forget that only one of them (the Count, as mere "Anlass" or occasion) had any hand in, and none of them does anything to avert, the tragic developments at the folk level which make the real substance of Brentano's tale. In this instance, the "lower-class plot" is so central that the upper-class plot can only obscure it. And the lower-class figures are the more convincingly drawn.

The ending is, moreover, unhappily moralistic. Grossinger's farewell letter and suicide are weak and anticlimactic. The placing of Annerl's apron in the ducal museum is a pedantic and chilling touch, as is the allegorical manipulation of the name "Voile de Grâce." The raising of the Duke's mistress in rank, and his reform and marriage, are reminiscent of Karl Eugen of Württemberg. Unhappiest of all is the somewhat *papier-mâché* monument to True and False Honor—as if these were so simply distinguishable, in any case! —which bear the likenesses of the Duke and the newly-created Duchess. One can only wish that Brentano had deleted this last page, for it merely serves to blur the simple lines of what he has so movingly portrayed, "die Tragik im Volke."

The most striking feature of style in *Kasperl und Annerl* is the use of a number of *leitmotifs* which are re-echoed and varied in pseudo-musical fashion, with compositional and "mood" values. This is a device which Otto Ludwig later used tellingly in *Zwischen Himmel und Erde*, he, too, long before the days of Thomas Mann, who has often been looked upon as the inventor of it. Anna Margaret's song of Judgment Day, "Ihr Toten, ihr Toten sollt auferstehn," is a solemn note that is struck again and again. The poor tinsel wreath, the "Kranz aus Flittergold," that Kasper brings from France for Annerl—a true example of folk-taste—and that shares his tragic fortunes, is seen last on the girl's severed head. Similarly, the "Schürze" or apron operates with sinister effect all through Annerl's life, becoming virtually a fate-tragedy "property." The recurrent phrase "es hat sie mit Zähnen dazu gerissen," which is used in varying formulations of Annerl (and once of Kasper), sums up the irresistible pull of fate on her. With grim understatement and ambiguity we are told several times of Kasper's "Abschied" or honorable discharge and of Annerl's "Ehrentag" or day of honor, which in each case, as we come to realize, means death without honor.[7]

More pleasing are the motifs of the rose and the veil, which amount to poetic symbols. The rose, given to Anna Margaret at the beginning of the story exactly on the spot where her lover gave her one seventy long years ago, is to her an earnest of imminent reunion with him in heaven. At the end, she pins her rose on the breast of the dead Annerl, where it again seems to symbolize, beyond death, life and love unending. With it is linked the rose-scented veil signifying "Gnade" or mercy, which is found by the narrator on the street, flutters as a pennant on Grossinger's sword on the futile ride, and covers Annerl's body and is buried with her, to whom it failed to bring mercy. Its burial seemingly signifies also the termination of the Duke's clandestine love-affair (123); it functions again to provide a title for the Countess, to whom it belonged, and it even has a place on the final monument. A song with lute accompaniment, inserted in the manner of Romantic narratives, interweaves with the veil the motifs of Gnade, Liebe, Ehre, and Rose (117).

The most important of all these recurrent motifs, and the one that imports the central ethical problem of the story, is "Ehre," Honor. The word is first spoken by the old woman near the outset, and from then on it occurs on nearly every page. The author-narrator soon admits his inability to give an adequate answer to this complex question: "Ich wollte, es sagte mir einmal einer etwas Hinreichendes darüber" (98). At the end, having exhibited various concepts and degrees of Honor, he seems to answer the question in terms of Anna Margaret's humble piety: the funeral sermon is to be preached on her favorite text, "Gebt Gott allein die Ehre" (123) and the memorial monument is to have the same purport (125).

The problem of honor, especially in its military formulation, figures in German literature from the days of the eighth-century *Hildebrandslied* to the time of Schnitzler.[8] Kasper, too, takes "honor" in the strictly military sense. It is exemplified for him in the anecdote he tells about a French officer who killed himself after being forced to commit a dishonorable act (97f.). This anecdote becomes Kasper's aegis and the pattern for his own end. Against it are measured other persons' conceptions of honor. Kasper's father and step-brother, soon to be unmasked as brigands, scoff at the story: "the man was a fool," judges the brother; "eat your 'honor,' if you are hungry," mocks the father. Whereupon Kasper takes up his sword (another symbol) and leaves his father's house forever. Anna Margaret, on the other hand, is moved by the anecdote, but she too speaks a different language. Her concept of "Ehre" is religious; she takes the word in at once the humblest and the highest sense: what is all human honor beside the honor we owe to God? So she says to her grandson "Gib Gott allein die Ehre!", echoing unconsciously the words of Meister Eckhart of five hundred years earlier: "gotes ist diu êre."

Kasper's estimation of honor has an element of ambition: his reputation and advancement in the army; it has an element of personal pride: he adjures Annerl not to dishonor him by marrying an inferior man after him (111). It is stern and merciless: "My honor does not permit me to spare anyone" (meine Ehre erlaubt mir keine Schonung), he says as he hands over his father and brother to the authorities (110). Yet this ideal, overwrought though it may be, is what lends him distinction, raises him above the anonymity of the crowd, and makes him a tragic figure. Like Kleist's Kohlhaas, this simple "Mann aus dem Volke" is a stalwart idealist; he cannot be bought off, he sees the thing through, cost what it may. He comes to grief, like Kohlhaas, because he carries a virtue to excess, insisting on an absolute in a world of moral relativities. Such men are commonly accounted fools, yet they are, self-consumed, humanity's beacons of uncompromising idealism in a world that is all too prone to selfish and craven compromise.[9]

Kasper's motivation is not blurred, as Annerl's is, by fate or magic. He is completely self-determining. Yet there is a touching spiritual kinship between the two lovers, not unlike that between Jude and his cousin in Hardy's novel. They come to suffer because they are finer than their kind. Even as a schoolboy, Kasper was superior: "Unter allen Burschen war er immer der reinlichste und fleissigste" (97). Similarly Annerl, who is exceptionally beautiful, "war immer feiner und manierlicher als alle andere Dirnen" (101). Out of a strict sense of honor, Kasper denounces his own family to the courts; in the same spirit, Annerl denounces herself. Both die for honor's sake, rejecting all compromise.

At first, to be sure, Annerl takes "Ehre" in the shallow sense of "Ehrsucht:" she affects finer dress and airs, and this weakness makes her an easier prey to the blandishments of a nobleman when she believes Kasper fallen in France. Her own guilt and suffering, however, deepen her nature, as they do that of Goethe's Gretchen. She rises to a high concept of honor that makes her unwilling to incriminate her seducer even to save her own life.[10] She burns up the written promise of marriage she has from him. Like Gretchen, she refuses rescue and insists on suffering the death penalty: "Ich habe sein Kind ermordet und will sterben und ihn nicht unglücklich machen; ich muss meine Strafe leiden, dass ich zu meinem Kinde komme" (117). This humble and unselfish resignation or "Ergebenheit in Gott" comes close to Anna Margaret's religious position, and it is utterly unjust to say or imply (as Brentano himself seems to do at the end) that Annerl represents "die falsche Ehre."

There can be no question, however, that for Brentano the chief significance of his story, above all its religious significance, is lodged in the old peasant woman of eighty-eight, Anna Margaret. She is the most impressive figure, and through her we see all the others, including the titular heroes, who do not appear to us directly at all.[11] Though she is nowhere specifically described, we seem to form a distinct picture of her; she constitutes perhaps the greatest triumph of Brentano's art of character-creation "überhaupt." From the very first glimpse of her he grants us, the author makes her imposing; there is "etwas sehr Befremdendes, ja schier Grosses" in her bearing, in her "wunderlich tiefen und ernsten Stimme" (91, 92). There is a solemn dignity about her that would make it inadmissible to apply an affectionate diminutive to her name, as is done with those of the title heroes. She is, when all is said and done, the real hero of the story she tells. She is continuously in view, and everything she does or says deeply affects her interlocutor and, through him, us. He is shaken (erschüttert) by her words (96), quite torn (ganz zerrissen) by her troubles; and the dignity and steadfastness (Grösse und Festigkeit) with which she bears them fill him with veneration (109). She speaks at times with a cryptic, almost mystic, solemnity: "Wenn ein Mensch fromm ist und hat Schicksale und kann beten," the relative trifles of life cannot vex him (92). Or she observes, with a paradox that is only apparent: "O, was läge am ganzen Leben, wenn's kein End' nähme? Was läge am Leben, wenn es nicht ewig wäre?" Or again, summing up heartbreaking experiences in the simplest of words: "Ach, das war wohl der schrecklichste Weg in meinem Leben" (109).

She is kept unsentimental, with much of the practical shrewdness of the peasant about her. She soberly pockets the coin given her (93). She refuses to grow sentimental over the changed world since she was young (94). She does not want pardon for Annerl, but justice; that, she says "coldly," is better than pardon (116). She speaks and weeps unsentimentally, coldly: "Sie weinte, ohne zu klagen, ihre Worte waren immer gleich ruhig und kalt" (101); "ganz ruhig" she relates and exhibits the most horrible things (109). At the end, after

Annerl's execution, she is oblivious of all the goings-on around her, concerned only for the decent laying-out of the body and the due observance of forms—a "volkstümlich" trait that we shall observe again in Barbara at the funeral in Grillparzer's *Spielmann*.

With Anna Margaret is connected what little humor there is —mostly of an unconscious and sometimes a grim sort—in this story, such as her naïve conception of the operations of a "writer" (101) or her quaint definition of a "Lehnerich" (100) or her strange account of a law that discriminates between suicides from melancholy and those from despair, the latter only being subject to dissection (111)!

In her unsentimental acceptance of adversity, in her native dignity and devoutness, Anna Margaret seems to personify the immemorial, anonymous, and inarticulate suffering of the peasantry, their infinite endurance, their seemingly inexhaustible spiritual resources. Amid all her troubles, she is sure that we get more mercies than we deserve in this life (100f.). Even in sufferings she sees divine benefactions, for God in His mercy sometimes sends us sorrow to countervail sorrow, as she puts it in the striking figure of the "Eisbrecher," the guard upstream of a bridge that wards off ice-floes from it: "Es war mir ein Stein vor das Herz gelegt, wie ein Eisbrecher, und alle die Schmerzen, die wie Grundeis gegen mich stürzten und mir das Herz gewiss abgestossen hätten, die zerbrachen an diesem Stein und trieben kalt vorüber" (112). This is the voice of Brentano's own mystical religious feeling, speaking from a creature of his unfulfilled longing. The spiritual stability which his life, peaceless from very childhood, denied him; the inner calm of uncomplicated and unquestioning faith for which he yearned, he personified in this simple old woman.

She represents also, one feels, the longing to escape from time. She herself seems to stand above time. She reminds us of Goethe's Manto: "Ich harre, mich umkreist die Zeit." In her long life she has seen the ageless themes of human existence return, unchanged beneath their ever-changing exteriors. On a May night such as this, seventy years ago, she, a country maid of eighteen, sat on this very doorstep, and a young soldier of the passing guard, in a uniform different from the present one, threw her a rose and she sang an old song. Now again the soldiers, the rose, and the song have come to her. Then her life was beginning, now it is ending, or rather, a new life is about to open beyond. And it all has seemed but a moment: "Es ist, als wenn man eine Hand umwendet" (94). Thus, in her detached view, life appears as a series of ever-closing circles. As her mind and memory range over this long period, so the story, largely because she tells it, interweaves somewhat startlingly events of the past, present, and future; for, as she says, "es ist doch alles einerlei" (95).

The world of *Kasperl und Annerl*, for all its massive realness, still trails the clouds of Romantic fancy from which it came. The reality here is still, on the whole, romanticized and unspecific. Kasperl and Annerl have about them something of the rigidity of figures in a tragic puppet-play. Anna Margaret herself is, on the whole, more legendary than real; she is cast in heroic size, with the magnified and timeless lineaments of myth. Nowhere do we get an indication of particular physical traits, beyond her deep voice; of her dress we see nothing but her big, black, oilcloth-covered hat and her apron, which is not further identified. When we compare this portraiture with that of Hauptmann's Bahnwärter Thiel, just seventy years later, we can measure the advance of Realism through the century. It is an ironical reflection that the less man comes to count for as an individual in modern mass life, the more carefully is he individuated in literature.

CHAPTER THREE

ARNIM, *DER TOLLE INVALIDE AUF DEM FORT RATONNEAU* (1818)

The knightly figure of Achim von Arnim does not stand in the first rank of German writers. Romantic enthusiast and Prussian patriot, richly endowed with poetic sensibility and fantasy, he was not equally gifted with self-criticism; and his healthy, harmonious nature lacked that passionate bias and intensity which distinguish the outright genius from the highly gifted amateur. Nevertheless, a few of Arnim's works have lived, chief among these the briefest, the story of a crazed French soldier who for three days and nights held a harbor fort single-handed and terrorized a city, but was saved from death and restored to sanity by the fearless love of his German wife.

This bare summary suggests at once some of the recognized characteristics of a Novelle: an extraordinary event that has actually occurred (Goethe's definition) and a story that can be condensed into a short sentence. And other earmarks of the Novelle are not lacking: the general brevity (in this case, less than twenty printed pages) and economy of structure, with everything built around the central "Ereignis" or conflict to which the action leads up and from which it falls away to its final resolution. Dispensing with a "frame," the author limits himself to a few crucial scenes which he presents vividly with a minimum of description, using a flexible combination of direct speech and indirect subjunctive discourse. There are in the center two chief characters, Francoeur and Rosalie, both mature and "fertig;" farther out, a few minor figures, more or less types: the old commandant, the man-servant, the priest; on the periphery, two or three individuals (the mother, the Leipzig pastor, the child—all three nameless) and the Marseilles populace. The action sets in, with dramatic emphasis, shortly before the catastrophe; then the past is revealed by means of a report which at the same time characterizes the two main persons. The time-span is short, the locale restricted and well defined. The only really dispensable elements are the brief pseudo-comical episode of the ignited wooden leg at the beginning, the touches of the supernatural connected with the mother, and the "tag" of two verses at the end, in which the author sums up for us in abstract, moralizing terms the theme and substance of his tale:

Gnade löst den Fluch der Sünde,
Liebe treibt den Teufel aus.

A "Falke" in Heyse's sense might be seen in the powder-tower about which the central action revolves; it is the source of Francoeur's dangerous power and at the same time a symbol of his explosive nature and soldierly character. A Tieckean "Wendepunkt" occurs in the middle of the narrative in the scene of the attempted exorcism, which sets Francoeur off on his fateful derangement. There are a number of leitmotifs: that of the Devil, that of the mother's curse, and others. The word "Teufel," in a variety of modulations, occurs about thirty times in this brief tale, the word and concept "Fluch" a dozen times. The color black recurs with a sinister suggestion of evil and supernatural forces. Rosalie, in an apprehensive mood, sees a "schwarze Fledermaus" spreading its opaque wings over her eyes (264).[1] Her mother appears to her inward eye "schwarz, mit flammenden Augen" (264). Francoeur develops an hallucination about black-robed clergymen (265, 270) and conceives the tormenting spirit in his head as a "Schornsteinfeger" or a "schwarzer Bergmann" (278). The motif of "Feuerwerk" is prominent also; the passion for fireworks connects Francoeur and the Commandant from the beginning; it helps to characterize the hero and it figures in the plot, for it is the reason why Francoeur is entrusted with the powder-magazine, and later on, the light from his rockets saves his wife and child from disaster (274). A lily-motif is connected with the heroine, whose maiden name was Lilie (262). She is identified in Francoeur's mind with the lily-flag of France that flies over the fort; and when in his frenzy he hauls down this flag to replace it by one with the Devil's likeness, he has broken both with his wife and his king (272, 276).

The use of these unifying motifs is consistent with the close-knit structure of the story as a whole. The action advances steadily and cogently, without gaps or pauses, with a certain military precision, and every step is adequately motivated. Arnim for once avoids all digressions and unnecessary embroidery and keeps to his main line. The strategic situation in the latter part, when Francoeur has taken sole command of the fort, is made clear, the tactical method in his madness being regarded with detached admiration by his opponents. From the quiet, idyllic beginning in the old Commandant's lodgings, the plot rises with increasing tension—retarded briefly by the happy interlude of the installation in the fort—to the sharp tragic climax of Francoeur's mad outbreak which threatens seemingly inescapable destruction for him and his little family and countless others. Then, the saving of the day by Rosalie's unflinching love and spiritual strength; then the rapid denouement, with an enthusiastic demonstration by the populace, and finally a quiet gathering-up of last threads.

This rise and fall is distinctly dramatic, and indeed there is a dramatic quality in the movement and gestures of the persons throughout; for example the excitable Francoeur's characteristic beating of his forehead (270, 278), the Commandant's turning away his eyes and dropping his voice as he tells Rosalie her husband's prospective fate (275), or Francoeur's sitting with eyes fixed on his wife and child during the painful probing of his wound (279). Individual scenes, like that between Francoeur and the bungling Basset, with its contrasting human types and speech and mounting excitement (269-271), are full of dramatic life. As a writer, Arnim was marked, like so many "Novellisten," by a combination of narrative and dramatic powers.

The language is correspondingly terse and vigorous. Sentences of a Kleistian compression and tension occur, such as the following: "So betrat sie den engen Felsgang, der, wie ein verlängerter Lauf, für zwei mit Kartätschen geladene Kanonen mit boshaftem Geize die Masse des verderblichen Schusses gegen die Andringenden zusammenzuhalten bestimmt war" (277). In moments of supreme emotion, the expression attains a deeply moving simplicity, as when Rosalie states her brave resolve to face her husband's rage: "Ich will den Teufel beschwören in ihm, ich will ihm Frieden geben, sterben würde ich doch mit ihm, also ist nur Gewinn für mich, wenn ich von seiner Hand sterbe, der ich vermählt bin durch den heiligsten Schwur" (276). Equally impressive is Francoeur's valedictory when, like the Prince of Homburg, he believes his life forfeited to the stern "Kriegsgesetz:" "Was ist Sterben? Starb ich nicht schon einmal, als du mich verlassen, und nun kommst du wieder, und dein Kommen gibt mir mehr, als dein Scheiden mir nehmen konnte, ein unendliches Gefühl meines Daseins, dessen Augenblicke mir genügen" (278).

In this Novelle, as in Brentano's, we can observe a blending of Romantic traditions with a new realism and an interest in abnormal psychology. The miraculousness and diabolism that lurk in the background still belong to Romanticism, but they are not allowed, except as psychological factors, to affect developments. The consistent and logical working-out of the physiological-psychological problem in the hero, culminating in the sober surgical explanation and procedure at the end (279), belongs to the new realism. In the mind of Rosalie we see at times a typical mixture of superstition and quite realistic considerations: "Jedesmal wenn ich ihm [Francoeur] erzählen wollte, dass ich durch den Fluch der Mutter vom Teufel besessen zu sein glaubte, schloss mir der Teufel den Mund, auch fürchtete ich, dass er mich dann nicht mehr lieben könne, dass er mich verlassen würde, und den blossen Gedanken konnte ich kaum überleben" (264f.).

At times Arnim overworks the miraculous element. It would have sufficed to let Francoeur's blood and tears extinguish his fuse, but in addition a gust of wind must blow the powder from the vents of his cannon and the devil-flag from the tower (278). The doves that come to the child are explained as household pets;[2] putting green leaves into their beaks makes them too obvious a symbol (278). The repentant mother's release by death on the very day of Rosalie's saving deed (279) is again too much of a "romantisches Wunder."

On the other hand the local color is authentic and quite in the spirit of Poetic Realism. On a visit to Southern France some years before, Arnim had acquainted himself with the actual terrain, so that here realism is supported by reality. His story abounds in realistic detail which has functional value. The coaches rolling up for the ball in the opening lines are kept in mind; on their return trip they serve to keep the Commandant and Basset awake, thus giving the servant a chance to eavesdrop on his master's thinking-aloud, from which the further developments ensue. The items of the fort's inventory are given, even to the names of its two-man garrison and the numbers of livestock. The beautiful view from this height, instead of being enlarged on, is dismissed with the ironical comment that the men are heartily tired of it and glad of a change of scenery (268). The details of the necessary renovation are seen with a practical eye, and the idyl of the first peaceful Sunday in the old fort is painted with as loving a "Kleinmalerei" as that of Riehl's later "kulturgeschichtliche Novelle" *Burg Neideck*. At every stage of Francoeur's "rebellion," which proceeds with the methodicalness characteristic of the man, we are shown with sharp realness the persons and also the things involved.

It is astounding what a wealth of characterization Arnim is able to compress within the limits of his brief Novelle. Francoeur, the hero, is to a large extent a type. At his first mention he is signalized as an exemplary soldier. He is esteemed as "the bravest and most resourceful of soldiers, the soul of the regiment" (262), and this character he keeps, despite all his mad pranks, which are ascribed both to the Devil and to his old head-wound. An "extraordinary soldier" (265), strict and conscientious in his new command (268), bristling in military pride (270), he is a blood-brother to Brentano's Kasperl.

Similarly "der gute alte Kommandant," introduced in the opening line, keeps this character throughout, and appears again in benevolent action as "der gute alte Kommandant" at the close. His wooden leg is "stock;" his penchant for fireworks, dramatically connected with it in the initial paragraph, gives him individual color, and various small traits round out his genial personality.[3]

His valet Basset, Francoeur's old friend, is deftly drawn. With his talkativeness and curiosity, his anxiety about his job, his well-intentioned meddling, his embarrassed voice "thin as a violin" (269), his timidity and consternation, he is a real individual and a sort of foil to the hero. Father Philip, another minor character, is both a type and an individual. Rosalie's mother is the only personage of whom we get merely an indirect characterization, for she does not appear in the story. She speaks to Rosalie in a dream, in somber riming language (a Romantic touch, 274); but though she contributes a weird "Stimmung" to the story, she remains a somewhat shadowy and not entirely credible figure. Her patriotic rage at her daughter's befriending of a foe, and her vengeful curse, are overdrawn. Yet in her connection with gambling and strange men—she finally elopes with a gambler (263, 264)—she is not without specific stamp.[4]

The most impressive figure in the story, however, and the chief bearer of its ethical import, is Rosalie. It is significant that when she is first mentioned, she is engaged in an act of helpfulness (261), and when her previous history is related, it begins with a deed of mercy and love toward a wounded enemy soldier (263). She personifies "charity" in its full complement of meanings. She belongs in the line of Genoveva and the maid in Hartmann's *Der arme Heinrich* and Gretchen and some of Wagner's heroines—the line of German women whose self-forgetful love has saved men's souls.

In contrast to the devil-motif which is at once connected with Francoeur, a saint-motif is linked with Rosalie from the beginning: when Francoeur first sees her, he insists there is a halo about her head (263). She gives up her mother, her friends, her country for the man she loves. The world turns against her, and she is driven out with her child like Genoveva or like Hagar (271). Yet she is by no means just an unworldly saint; she is a clear-eyed, resolute woman who comprehends the practical situation, deliberately decides what must be done, and does it with steadfast courage. She confronts the Commandant with argument and accusation (274). Her moral strength lies in her utter unselfishness and piety. Having overcome her fear, she faces her ordeal unsentimentally and calmly, "in aller Ruhe eines gottergebenen Gemütes" (276). She is illuminated by an inner faith which tells her that what sustains this day's test will live immortally, and she grieves more for her husband and child than for herself (277). Her fidelity and her faith, "Treue und Ergebenheit in Gott," bring about the final solution (279).

The two chief figures have a national representative value and afford an effective contrast: Francoeur with his French excitability and martial spirit and dash, triumphantly acclaimed by "a people who always prize boldness more than goodness;"[5] Rosalie with her German faithfulness and self-subordination and "Fraulichkeit." They supplement each other excellently, and anticipate the German-French pair in Clara Viebig's Novelle *Der Gefangene*, embodying in their way a like preachment of international understanding and cooperation which is the more striking as coming from so thorough a Prussian as Arnim and so soon after the great war with France.

The brevity and trained-down "leanness" of Arnim's story bring it close to the line of the "Anekdote." On the other hand the depth of character-drawing here, the scope of the action, and its general human significance, keep it well within the range of the true Novelle. In contrast, Kleist's *Bettelweib von Locarno*, which is commonly considered a Novelle, is by strict definition an anecdote, for it lacks just that depth of motivation and that correspondence of character with fate, which distinguish Arnim's story. Arnim, however, learned much from Kleist, even more than Brentano did, and his masterpiece, *Der tolle Invalide*, bears unmistakably the stamp of that great forerunner of 19th-century realism and novellistic art.

CHAPTER FOUR

ANNETTE VON DROSTE-HÜLSHOFF,
DIE JUDENBUCHE (1842)

Annette von Droste-Hülshoff, the greatest woman poet whom Germany has produced, lived a lonely and unnoticed life. She was as little regarded by her age as was her great contemporary in the South, Eduard Mörike. Both of them published a first collection of poems in 1838, and each sold well under one hundred copies. Annette, like Mörike, did not fit into any of the categories of contemporary literature, and has proved difficult to "classify" since. She had some residual traits of Romanticism; on the other hand she anticipated to an amazing extent, like Büchner, the Naturalism of a much later period. She was a strikingly original and independent writer. Toward the literary developments of her own time, the 1830's and 1840's, dominated as they were by tendentious social and political "poetry," she took a critical and negative attitude, and she expressly eschewed fame in her lifetime. Yet, isolated though she was by her nature, her sex, and her conservative family and religion from many of the new intellectual currents in those years of transition from Romanticism to Realism, she could not remain unaffected by them; she was herself, without plan or intent, a part of that very transition and of the Poetic Realism into which it flowered. When, in conscious opposition to the Romantic tradition (einer gewissen romantischen Schule), she insisted that her forte was the faithful but poetically refined reproduction of Nature (dass ich nur im Naturgetreuen, durch Poesie veredelt, etwas leisten kann),[1] she accredited herself as a Poetic Realist in the very heyday of Young Germany.

Annette wrote only one Novelle, *Die Judenbuche,* but it is both a masterpiece of its genre and an early monument of Poetic Realism. It possesses the earmarks established by theorists and practitioners as characteristic of the Novelle. It has a prominent central "event," in Goethe's sense of "eine sich ereignete, unerhörte Begebenheit." It has an "idea," which could be stated most briefly in Chaucer's "mordre wol out," or in the phrase "die Sonne bringt es an den Tag," which forms the burden of the related *Märchen* of the Grimms and of Chamisso's poem. It has a splendid "falcon" in the beech tree which gives the story its name and its focal center. As a thing of Nature, unfeeling, removed from human life, the "Buche" is a mute and awesome symbol of those superhuman forces of divine retribution or Fate which at this very time Stifter was struggling to understand and accept. The peculiar village world of the story, with its motifs of forest and timber-poaching, its communal activities and prejudices and superstitions, shows that definite individual stamp which Heyse designated as a "Silhouette." Besides *the* Beech, other trees of the forest figure as symbolic motifs: the beech, felled in full leaf (16),[2] which represents the ruthless "timber-crimes" (Holzfrevel), or the Broad Oak under which Hermann Mergel died and which his unshriven spirit haunts (12, 16). A characterizing leitmotif is the strange glassy lustre that comes over the hero's eyes in moments of passion (18, 23, 24). The scene of his public humiliation by the Jew, which motivates the slaying of the latter, provides the "turning-point" which Tieck considered essential.

Only a small number of persons are involved in the central action, but these are not only adults, whose already fixed characters are tested in the fire of an extraordinary event; for in the hero a whole lifetime is brought before us, from birth to death, fifty years and more—in fact, even the determinative conditions preceding his birth are clearly set forth. In other words, Annette has conquered a new field for the Novelle, a field traditionally reserved for the novel: the depiction of a personality in its entire scope and growth, its "Werden und Wesen," and its "Umwelt" or social *milieu*. *Die Judenbuche* constitutes a modern enlargement of the Novelle which, by analogy to the great German tradition of the "Entwicklungsroman," the novel of development, might well be called an "Entwicklungsnovelle:" though the conflict of a matured individual with society forms the climax of the story, we are shown the development of the hero up to this crisis, and on to his end. We see organically unfolding in him the qualities of character which will make him a mark for Fate. This prodigious condensation is made possible by a technique of scene-sequence, a series of dramatic pictures which give us glimpses of significant turning-points; a brilliant anticipation of the art of the cinema, illuminating only parts of the action and yet creating the illusion of continuity and completeness. We shall observe this same procedure later in Storm's *Schimmelreiter;* but Annette's compression is even greater than his, and anticipates him by half a century.

She gives her story an appearance of documentary truth like that of Kleist's *Michael Kohlhaas,* fulfilling the "sich ereignete" proviso of Goethe's definition. All the way through she notes exact dates. She allows the Brandes-Blaukittel development to come to a dead end, and enters her story with a sole "ich" to explain that it would be reprehensible in the case of an invented tale thus to disappoint the reader's expectation; but this is a true story, with nothing added and nothing taken away (31). And at the end she solemnly asseverates: "This is an account, with all the essential details, of what actually happened in September of the year 1789" (53).

As a true realist, she aims at complete objectivity of report. She prefaces her story in an unusual way with a twelve-line poem which at once states her theme, sets a serious tone, and expresses her subjective attitude, which is one of sympathy, like Hauptmann's, for underprivileged and stunted lives. The poem, like the story itself in effect, is a preachment on the text: let the fortunate not cast stones. This sentiment of Christian charity contrasts strangely with the harsh Old Testament ethics later exemplified, yet both poem and story reflect a very modern awareness of the social factors—hereditary, environmental, educational—that determine character and "guilt."

Having thus as it were segregated her personal feelings in the introductory verses, the author maintains, in the story proper, an eminently objective and detached, even ironical, relation to her persons. She does not, any more than Kleist did, withhold her opinions: an editorial "we" occurs twice (8, 28), shrewd generalizing comments on human nature several times (11, 12, 13, 46), and once there is a summarizing analysis of the hero (32-33). But such interpolations are always spiced with an irony which preserves the objectivity of the author. She ironizes her hero's complacent thoughts (18), his performance as a fiddler and dancer (34-35), his "gallant" toast to the gentry (35), his stage-effect with the watch (36). She ironizes Margret's human weakness for self-deception (20) and her conviction of the pricelessness of her own counsel (21). Annette pictures her Westphalian peasants with irony (34, 36), and points out that Aaron's grief-stricken widow soon comforted herself with a new husband (43).

The limited compass of the Novelle sets a high premium on succinct characterization, and in this art Annette proves herself a master. She not only gives a life-length portrait of the hero, but makes a number of other figures, both central and incidental, phenomenally vivid. We get a clear idea of Margret, though her exterior is nowhere described, except for the detail of her being deaf in the right ear—a detail which, characteristically, is revealed in action, not static statement (17). Honest, upright, well-intentioned, but without "horizon" and with the prejudices of her kind, which she passes on to her son; poor, helpless, and ready to rationalize unavoidable evil to make it acceptable; a pious woman, persuading herself that the prophylaxis of daily prayer will preserve her son from the contamination of her brother's sinister world. An average person, like her son, she becomes truly tragic in her collapse after his crime and flight: a deeply moving study in human deterioration.

Simon's outward appearance is described in a very few lines when he first comes on: small, lean, restless, with fishy eyes and a face like a pike's, he alternates pompous mysteriousness with affected candor—certainly a man to make one feel uneasy (ein unheimlicher Geselle, 12). He is linked with the outer atmosphere of weirdness that surrounds this realistic tale. In his person, the folk-motif of the Devil, first introduced in the impatient words of Margret (9) and strengthened by the transformation of old Mergel into a malevolent spirit (12), enters the action bodily: Simon, departing with Friedrich, his coat-tails like fiery flames behind him, is quite clearly clad in the livery of Hell (14) —this is the Evil One going off with a recruit, "ihn meine Strasse sacht zu führen," and the family likeness of the two only affirms the ghastly fact that heredity, too, works for the Devil.

Simon's unacknowledged son, Johannes Niemand, is another significant addition of Annette's to her source. In his uncanny resemblance to the hero, he represents a new formulation of the mirror-motif which figures in Annette's poetry as a symbol for the deceptive appearances of things,[3] the baffling duplicity of life and of human nature. Like Medardus and his double in Hoffmann's *Elixiere des Teufels*, Johannes serves both to incriminate and to exculpate the hero. And, having served his purpose, he vanishes. He is merely mentioned, a half-year after Friedrich's flight, as a sort of ditto-mark: "Friedrich had disappeared and—Johannes Niemand, the poor, unnoticed Johannes, on the same day as he" (44). At the end, Friedrich as it were steps into his shoes, and Johannes's final fate is nowhere recorded.

Aside from these three central figures there are a number of outlying ones, they, too, clearly drawn: Hermann Mergel, the "decent drunkard" (ordentlicher Säufer), his character and ten years of his married life compressed into less than two pages of print (7-9); the choleric Forester Brandes, the plodding Court Clerk Kapp, the canny neighbor Hülsmeyer, the Jew Aaron and his wife, and, delineated with special affection, the local nobleman and his lady, who are somewhat reminiscent of the author's parents. Even purely peripheral figures, like the peasant bridal couple (36), are individualized with a few adroit lines—a neat little vignette "am Rande." At the end of the story, the Hülsmeyer family is brought in again (45ff.), instead of a new family's being introduced for the purpose. This is typical of the economy of Annette's Novelle, and in this way, one may say, a circle is closed, with the effect of knitting the whole closer together. The village swineherd is silhouetted in just one line earlier in the story; his son comes to occupy Margret's house after her death (36, 47). Brandes is succeeded as Forester by his son (47), who appropriately brings about the denouement, thus closing another circle (52f.). After many years, the returned fugitive's story bears out Kapp's account (41, 48). Friedrich's knack at woodcarving (23) figures again much later in his spoon-making (49). The ill-assorted pair at the peasant wedding recalls the ill-matched parents of the hero. At the first "Haussuchung," the fateful silver watch is found at the bottom of Friedrich's trunk (40); at the second search, again conducted by the Baron, the house has been reduced to a room, the trunk to a small cardboard box, the watch to four little silver buttons (51)—all emblematic of the decline in Friedrich's fortunes. The meaning of the Hebrew inscription on the tree—which the author counts on our not being able to read—is kept a secret until the very last line of the story, whence it casts a revealing light backward upon the earlier action. The extraordinary likeness of the cousins, prepared for at the beginning, makes possible a startling effect of disclosure at the end. And the widest circle of all closes with the finding of Friedrich's body hanging in the tree under which he had slain the Jew twenty-eight years before.

In her treatment of Nature, Annette employs, besides some lingering Romanticism, the more realistic manner of a newer age. She still senses the old irrational mystery of the "Wald;" she even echoes Tieck's magical word "Waldeinsamkeit" (6).

She can still indulge in the "pathetic fallacy:" B. Castle is described as looking down with grey and distinguished air upon the village huts, which like old consumptive folk seem ever about to collapse but continue to stand (44). Yet Annette does not romanticize or humanize the crucial Beech—as even Otto Ludwig likes to do with trees and shrubs—nor does she use it for lyrical "Stimmung" or atmosphere; she leaves it a real thing of Nature, even though the inscription on it has marked it with human significance.

Throughout the story, we are made aware of the natural background of every scene. But the description is never an end in itself, and is held to the utmost brevity. Nature has "mood value" but also functional importance in the human action. Man is still set in Nature, adjusted to it; but in a practical way. The forest, for example, is not the object of dreamy contemplation; it figures realistically as a means of livelihood for the villagers. A severe January snowstorm is a very natural cause for an inebriated man, returning through the woods at night, to lose his way and his life (9-10). Christmas Eve is a natural time for one who has been long years away to want to reach home; beyond this, to be sure, there are deep poetic and "romantic" overtones in this wonderful black-and-white picture (44-45). There is more of the traditional "Nature-background" in the use of a violent thunder-storm as the setting for Friedrich's crime and flight, or in the briefly indicated autumn scene for the ending of his life: stripped fields, falling leaves, and Death also preparing to reap its harvest (50). There is in fact an autobiographical relevance in the fixing on the equinox, for that was always a critical time for Annette herself. On the other hand, we feel an entirely impersonal quality in the setting for the final unpleasant revelations: a late-summer day; air vibrating with heat, no birds singing, only crows cawing heavily in the branches and opening their beaks to the sultry air—again only three lines of description (52).

In all this we see the Romantic love of "Naturstimmung" being tempered by a sober sense of fact. That the Nature here depicted is the author's familiar native heath is another element characteristic of Poetic Realism, for that movement was intimately linked with the development of regional art or "Heimatkunst."[4]

Quite in the manner of Poetic Realism is the careful recording of the particulars of everyday living in cottage and castle, in field and forest—interiors as well as outdoor activities are vividly brought to view, but with the subtle artistic selection that distinguishes the Poetic Realist, and with the succinctness imposed by the restricted compass of the Novelle. Thus the former prosperity of the Mergel house is indicated by its chimney and extra-large window-panes; its deterioration by the neglected fence, the damaged roof, and the unweeded garden with its woody, unpruned rosebushes (7). A little masterpiece of atmosphere and tension is the daybreak picture that precedes the murder of Brandes: the nature-scene, Friedrich and his every expression and movement, the sounds of birds and man, even the characteristic behavior of a sleeping dog hit by a stone (23). Then the details of the Forester's movements as he "fades out" in the undergrowth: his professional gait, the branches closing behind him, the glint of his uniform-buttons, the click of his flint (25). A few details of furnishings convey the oppressive atmosphere of Friedrich's shabby little room (51). A few realistic traits make up the unsentimental portrait of the peasant bridal couple (36).

At the end of the story, Poetic Realism passes over into what a later period would have called outright Naturalism. Our noses are assailed by the stench of putrefying human flesh, and our eyes by the sight of maggots at work in it. Annette follows her hero through to the "Schindanger" or carrion-pit that receives his reduced remains, and finishes factually with the exact date on which all this was done.

With all her lucid realism, however, she has left an aura of mystery about her tale. In the sunlit village life there is at times a strange blurring of perception, not only of moral values but of actual happenings. Many of these are never cleared up; no one seems to know who was where or did what. The Blue-Coats and their well-organized enterprise vanish suddenly like shadows. Johannes drops out of the story without explanation or epitaph, Simon is everywhere and nowhere. His craft and power are great, yet he appears but briefly, and never in full lighting. A good deal of the story runs underground, like a lost river; only parts of its course are in full view. Much of the psychological motivation is eliminated or "covered" by the fact that the returned Friedrich is taken by the villagers to be Johannes, and deliberately lives the part which chance has assigned to him. We do not know what is going on in his mind, and the author could not tell us without giving away her plot; we get only surface manifestations—a furtive glance, a slashed spoon (50-51)[5]—of the inner forces that drive this man to his doom. The fact that he lives behind a mask and cannot confide in anyone is doubtless one of the psychic pressures that bring him to the fated tree at last.

Annette's style, both in narrative and lyric, is distinctly pictorial: every matter resolves itself for her into a series of pictures or scenes. Her work in ballads and lyrics, her religious poetry at its best, and her epics in prose and verse, all share this picture-quality or "Bildhaftigkeit." She had a dramatic *anlage*, too; she evinces a marked stage-sense, a power to visualize her persons' every movement and facial expression, and to hear their speech. Like Conrad Ferdinand Meyer, she attempted drama without success, but had to a high degree the capacity of scene-seeing; she was, like him, an "eidetic." It is her marvellous scene-technique that enables her to compress into a fifty-page Novelle the substance of a novel.

She instinctively vivifies even small, incidental action. Johannes-Friedrich's landlady reports him missing. The Baron expresses concern; his voice rises as he orders out searchers, as he thinks excitedly (bewegt) of increasingly serious things that might have befallen the cripple. "Take the dogs along," he calls after the departing men, "and look in the ditches," and, raising his voice still louder, "—and in the quarries!" (50).

In moments of tension, the sentences—at no time involved—become notably brief and dramatic, with emphasis on verbs of action. "Friedrich ward still; er horchte noch ein Weilchen und schlief dann ein. Nach einigen Stunden erwachte er. Der Wind hatte sich gewendet. . . . Die Mutter richtete sich auf; das Toben des Sturms liess einen Augenblick nach. Man hörte deutlich an den Fensterläden pochen und mehrere Stimmen: 'Margret! Frau Margret, heda, aufgemacht!' Margret stiess einen heftigen Laut aus! 'Da bringen sie mir das Schwein wieder!' Der Rosenkranz flog klappernd auf den Brettstuhl, die Kleider wurden herbeigerissen. Sie fuhr zum Herde, und bald darauf hörte Friedrich sie mit trotzigen Schritten über die Tenne gehen. Margret kam gar nicht wieder" (9-10).

One might say that *Die Judenbuche* consists of twelve to fifteen scenes, with a little connective matter between them. After indicating the prenatal factors that are to determine her hero's life, and announcing his birth, the author jumps to his ninth year and a particular night at Epiphany. After a few lines of explanation, the scene develops in action and dialogue, wonderfully terse and lifelike (9-10). The next scene is two days later, after the father's burial, a brief but important dialogue of mother and son, during which dubious concepts of right and wrong, of law and property, and of racial prejudice are instilled in the questioning child's mind (11). The next scene occurs three years later, when Friedrich is twelve years old, and introduces the third main character, Ohm Simon (12ff.). If we observe Margret in this colloquy, we see that the author records her motions and emotions in virtual stage-directions; Margret trembles, she clutches the back of a chair, she sighs, blushes furiously with annoyance, drops her voice, is touched to tears, smiles with secret pride, breaks a branch from the hedge and steps forward to meet her son, feigning to help him drive in the cows, but really whispering a word of warning to him—all this in about one page of print. We are reminded of the way in which Kleist accompanies speech with gesture introduced by "indem."

This scene passes into a peripatetic one as Simon and the boy walk through the moonlit woods (15-17). An eerie "Stimmung" is engendered by the intermittent light and fleeting shadows; the moon is in its first quarter, and its feeble rays make everything seem weird and wavering to Friedrich's excited fancy. The dialogue is somewhat one-sided, Simon sounding out his nephew as to his suitableness for Simon's ulterior purposes. For all its artistically sustained mood, the scene is marked by sharply observed details of actuality.

In the next scene (17ff.) we are back in Margret's house, and we experience with her the uncanny interplay of semblance and reality as she comes upon Friedrich's "double" crouched over her kitchen fire, effectively lighted by the flames: her child and yet not her child! Again the author supplies a complete set of "stage-directions" for the movement, gesture, facial expression, and speech of all three persons.

After an interval of comment, we get our next glimpse of Friedrich at eighteen (22-26). The curtain rises on July 11, 1756, at three in the morning, in the woods. Friedrich in his "other" role as a ragged cowherd, on guard for the Blue-Coats;

the coming of dawn, the entry of Brandes and his rangers, with detailed pantomime; excited dialogue, with consummate "acting" on Friedrich's part: gestures, changes in face and voice, honest rage giving way to cold vengefulness; his dumb-play and few words after Brandes' exit—all this makes vivid drama, tense with emotion but objectively staged, with two diametrically different temperaments pitted against each other.

There follows immediately an interior scene in the Mergel house, on the afternoon of the same day (26-28): Friedrich in bed, his mother, a neighbor, Kapp, Johannes—again completely visualized in action and speech. After a few lines of connection, the scene of the inquest (28-31): a crowded courtroom, testimony of witnesses, dramatic production of the *corpus delicti*, again cool acting by Friedrich. The brief scene that next follows (31-32), after an explanatory paragraph, is one of the most brilliant in the story, a weird *chiaroscuro* full of shifting shadows and moonlight and tense whispers. It marks the last rebellion of Friedrich's conscience; it is a duel of wills in which he succumbs to Simon's hardened depravity. A page of comment, and then the next scene (33-36), which brings us to the climax. Four years have passed; Friedrich is now twenty-two. Again the exact date is given: October 1760. A wedding in the village. Friedrich in all his glory as the leading dandy, and then deflated and disgraced by the behavior of Johannes. A still more crushing humiliation follows outside, while we are occupied with the peasant wedding "on stage:" the Jewish trader Aaron reclaims Friedrich's watch, which has not been paid for. Out of this grows the nocturnal encounter in the woods and Aaron's death. Both these "scenes," curiously enough, Annette puts offstage, though we get vivid reports of them and actual snatches of dialogue.

After two minor scenes (38-40): one in the castle three days later, with the announcement of the slaying and the finding of Aaron's body; the other the brief and pathetic one of the searching of Friedrich's room—comes another scene of extraordinary power (44-45): the culprit's homecoming after twenty-eight years of slavery and exile. Once more the time is fixed with documentary preciseness: it is the evening of December 24, 1788. The landscape background: the deep snow and intense cold, the solitary, weary figure coming over the hill, pausing to take in the miracle of the lights of home in the valley below; the old

Christmas hymn swelling on the still air, the wayfarer falling to his knees, overcome with remorse and gratitude (we infer), sobbing and praying—this would be, purely as a painting, impressive; but when considered in all its implications for plot and characterization, it is a supreme artistic achievement, one of the greatest scenes in German narrative literature. The author maintains her reticent objectivity: she does not analyze, she sets a person before us, reports his actions, and lets us draw our own conclusions.

After this high-point there follow a number of lesser dramatic scenes: "Johannes," a tragic Rip Van Winkle, being interrogated by the villagers; "Johannes" at the castle, telling his story to the Baron, the prematurely aged derelict and the still youthful old nobleman clearly contrasted in appearance, manner, and speech. Then, after a few little pictures, the final denouement (52-53), beginning as usual with a specification of the time: "two weeks later . . ." and proceeding in climactic disclosures to the last.

The ethical problem with which the author is concerned is that of crime and punishment. But in contrast to older, simpler ideas of guilt and atonement, "Schuld und Sühne," as exemplified, say, by Schiller, Annette writes with an eye to social conditions, above all, the forces of heredity and environment. Departing radically from her "source," a slight and external tale entitled *Geschichte eines Algierer Sklaven,* she passes over the long years of the hero's bondage almost in silence and instead, from the very beginning, she emphasizes the man's "Vorgeschichte"—how he came to be what he is. In the successive reworkings of her manuscript she eliminated—even to the point of eventual obscurity in some places[6]—almost everything that did not bear directly on the development of her hero from birth to death, and she even considered prenatal influences. In her final revision, only the peasant-wedding scene and some of the doings in the "Schloss" (recorded with filial fondness) could strictly be called dispensable to the ideal "leanness" of the Novelle.

The carefully detailed picture of the young hero's "Umwelt" is Annette's most significant addition to her source. Her approach, through ever-narrowing circles of environment, is comparable to that of a motion-picture. It is plain from her prefatory poem that she means to deal with one of the obscure and under-privileged. She begins, indeed, with her hero's name and birthdate;

but then, far from signalizing him as an extraordinary individual —as Kleist does in the opening sentence of *Michael Kohlhaas*— she depicts the social setting out of which grew this inconspicuous "Menschenkind" Friedrich Mergel. His very name is descriptive, for "Mergel" means marl, a kind of earth. Layer by layer, the author exposes the conditions that, even before the child was born or conceived, determined the man's character and fate.

First, our attention is focused on the province (Ländchen) of which his native town is a part; then, the dubious moral "climate" and the "working" ethical code of the time and place into which he is cast: the "law" of public opinion, of custom, of superannuation which has grown up like an indistinguishable weed beside the none too vigorous plant of the legitimate law. Then the racial type, the "Menschenschlag," of this region and its conflict with the authorities—which is more a matter of war between equals, waged with like weapons, than the rule of an ethic recognized as superior. Then the particular village, its natural setting, its bold temper, its particular form of cooperative lawbreaking: timber-theft, carried on as a communal venture, the chief magistrate (Ortsvorsteher) himself leading the nocturnal raids with the same pride with which he takes his seat in the courtroom. The whole male population, from striplings to septuagenarians, sets out boldly with thirty to forty carts on a fine moonlight night, much like a night-shift of legitimate factory workers. Here, clearly, wrong-doing is accepted and respectable. This is the established moral sea-level from which the hero starts.

Then the camera turns upon Friedrich's birthplace: his parents' house, a picture of decay given in a "flash" of utmost brevity, but in character very much like the more extensive one in Keller's *Romeo und Julia*. Then we are shown, with an unsentimental realism sharpened by irony, the parents themselves: Mergel, the ne'er-do-well, his miscarried first marriage, his decline to a worthless wretch (verkommenes Subjekt, 7); Margret, over-old, selfrighteous and selfconfident; then the gradual deterioration of this second marriage, into which, late and unwanted, this foredoomed child is born.

In less than four pages, Annette has thus given us a complete and overwhelming picture of the suprapersonal forces that determine individual lives. It is clear that she means to ascribe a good part of her hero's guilt to social factors beyond his control. This is a new departure in the history of German fiction. It serves to remind us that we are here in the Post-Romantic age of Hegel and of new, collective, racial conceptions of history and morality that have supplanted the individualism of the "Goethe-Zeit." The world of *Die Judenbuche* is a far cry from the age of Idealism and the moral freedom of Schiller's heroes; indeed, it anticipates by a half-century the social ethics of Naturalism.

Friedrich's early development represents almost a modern case study of the neglected child. He grows up in an unhappy household. His mother gives him affection, but no intelligent guidance. He soon loses his father, who, hardened though he was toward everyone else, had a special tenderness for his little son. When Hermann is brought home dead, no one explains to the child; someone "quiets" him with a box on the ear, and he has to pick up from chance remarks the tragic fact of his loss. His mother brings him up over-tenderly, cherishing his golden curls and training him to play the part of a daughter to an ailing widow (14). The uncle, who might have supplied a salutary male influence, is anything but a desirable mentor.

The boy naturally identifies himself with his father, yet has to hear the latter's memory constantly aspersed by others; this marks the beginning of an anti-social resentment and aggressiveness in him. Rebuffed by his fellows in defending his father's reputation, he becomes a solitary, herding cows in remote places, regarded as spiteful and secretive (13). A few years later, while continuing to indulge in this somewhat juvenile occupation, he develops, again under social pressure, a new side to his nature: a sense of inferiority, a desire for public acceptance (Geltung) lead him to ostentation in clothes and behavior. So he is seen in a double role, now dressed-up and jovial as the recognized village dandy and leader of the young folk, and then again a ragged herdboy, a lonely day-dreamer in fields and woods (21).

His family inheritance shows in both these propensities. The power of heredity as fate is symbolized in Friedrich's uncanny resemblance to his uncle as he follows in his footsteps, his eyes fixed on him with a weird fascination, as though in a magic mirror he were regarding with dismay his own inescapable future (15). Both the ostentation and the secretiveness which appear in Friedrich were already pointed out in the uncle, and if Simon has a face "wie ein Hecht (pike)," Friedrich tosses his head "wie ein Hecht" as he dances (12, 35).

Friedrich is always seen in relation to public opinion. He "puts on" as a defense against social disapproval. His sensitive egoism makes him aware of the covert opposition of some of the important people, so he is always under arms, ready not so much to defy public opinion openly as to steer it subtly in his favor (33); this oblique attack is quite characteristic of him. The disgrace which Johannes indirectly brings upon him by his petty thieving is a great blow to Friedrich's social prestige; this motivates his harshness to his protégé and, as further "compensation," his display of the watch; this in turn calls forth Hülsmeyer's jibe and prepares for the even more shameful scene with Aaron (35-37).

We see, then, the whole series of influences and mischances which plotted the career of this man and raised him, through no inherent quality of greatness either in good or in evil, into such dubious prominence. *Die Judenbuche* shows us the temptation and guilt of an entire community brought to a head in one of its members.[7] Friedrich Mergel is no salient, heroic individual such as the previous literature knew; no Wallenstein or Guiskard challenging Fate, but an ordinary specimen of his kind, a man in whom good and bad are mixed, a product of the standards and prejudices of his time and place, who might have "gone right" as readily as wrong—for his nature, as well as his features, does not lack nobility (33). He is conditioned by clan and community. Everything he does, up to the killing of the Jew, is within the *mores* of his group. The wholesale timber-thefts are no crime according to the local code, but part of a pseudo-legal class warfare. The murder of the Forester, to which Friedrich is an accessory (though he meant only to send Brandes to a beating, not to his death), is "tolerated" by the village, and in its stubbornly maintained anonymity it remains a communal act. A severe beating of the Jew and cheating him of his claim would likewise have been countenanced.[8] Only the actual slaying, as a private and individual deed, "goes too far" and makes Friedrich a marked man in the position of Manz and Marti in Keller's *Romeo und Julia*, the chance "conductor" of a crime that any fellow-citizen might have committed.[9]

Beyond this persuasive exposition of the social determinants of right and wrong, however, *Die Judenbuche* adumbrates a larger, indeed a cosmic problem of Evil. The moral issue of the story is not so much one of Old Testament ethics (despite the fulfilment of the Hebrew inscription), nor so much one of Fate in the Greek sense, as it is the demonstration of Man's moral frailty and defenselessness in a baffling and inimical world. For, when all is said and done, the punishment in this case does not fit the crime. Outwardly, Friedrich's suicide exemplifies the retributory justice of "an eye for an eye, a tooth for a tooth" which Aaron's widow invokes. Inwardly, it is a completely amoral solution, like the killing of a hunted animal. The quality of Christian mercy that rings in the Christmas song and brings the homing penitent to his knees in the snow has no part whatever in his final treatment. Long years of bitter hardship in exile have strained his endurance to the human limit.[10] The love of home and loyalty to his ancestral faith have brought this cripple back over incredible distances; and he, who in his pride and vanity once took a human life, has now, broken in body and spirit, dropped into the humble role of his "other self," become in effect a harmless half-wit, doing what he can for good. But there is no mercy in Heaven and no expiation through suffering. The mask that deceives his fellow-men does not hide Friedrich from the sleepless eyes of those vindictive powers to whom he could have cried, like Goethe's despairing Harper:

> Ihr führt ins Leben uns hinein,
> Ihr lasst den Armen schuldig werden,
> Dann überlasst ihr ihn der Pein:
> Denn alle Schuld rächt sich auf Erden.

One may say, then, that Annette's attempt to solve the problem of guilt and punishment in terms of human justice, with reference to man's social conditionedness, is wrecked upon her recognition of the moral blindness of life itself. The stark cruelty of the ending of *Die Judenbuche* is predicated upon the savagery of life and of the dark forces that shape it. Friedrich's crime was unpremeditated and unwilled;[11] it was not murder, but manslaughter in a quarrel, in hot blood, and human courts would normally have considered it cancelled by the passage of time (as in fact it was in Annette's source) as well as by the culprit's severe sufferings and present condition. For this deed, notwithstanding—with utter exclusion of the religious offices of confession and atonement—he is driven to suicide, thus adding to an ordinary crime a mortal sin—a conclusion that is surely amazing when considered as the work of a woman and a professed Catholic, and that makes sense only on the supposition that life is at its core irrational and beyond human understanding.

Annette's Novelle is thus an unusually characteristic example of the "Welt- und Kunstanschauung," the philosophical and artistic principles, of Poetic Realism. For though it is a "true story," presenting a complete and convincing picture of social facts and forces, the author does not stop at these in the manner of Determinism or of Existentialism; she imposes a pattern on them, she views them in relation to a higher and wider frame of reference: both her own metaphysical convictions and the sovereign powers of poetic re-creation that raise bare factuality to true reality.

CHAPTER FIVE

STIFTER, *ABDIAS* (1842)

One of the modern theorists of narrative literature, Georg Lukács, has evolved a view of the Novelle for which Adalbert Stifter's *Abdias* seems a perfect illustration. The Novelle, says Lukács, is "the embodiment of the isolated remarkableness and dubiousness of life . . . . The strident arbitrariness of Chance, beneficent or destructive, but always striking irrationally, can be balanced only by a clear, purely objective comprehension of it, without comment. The Novelle is the most purely artistic of forms; the ultimate meaning of all artistic creation is expressed by it as mood, as the substantial meaning of form-giving, even though, for that very reason, abstractly expressed. [The writer of the Novelle,] viewing the naked, unembellished senselessness of life, lends to it, by virtue of the magical power of this fearless and hopeless gaze, the consecration of form: the senselessness takes shape as senselessness; it has become eternal, affirmed by form, cancelled out, and redeemed" (die Form der isolierten Merkwürdigkeit und Fragwürdigkeit des Lebens . . . Die schreiende Willkür des beglückenden oder vernichtenden, aber immer grundlos darniederfahrenden Zufalls kann nur durch sein klares, kommentarloses, rein gegenständliches Erfassen balanciert werden. Die Novelle ist die am reinsten artistische Form; der letzte Sinn alles künstlerischen Formens wird von ihr als Stimmung, als inhaltlicher Sinn des Gestaltens, wenn auch eben deshalb abstrakt, ausgesprochen. Indem die Sinnlosigkeit in unverschleierter, nichts beschönigender Nacktheit erblickt wird, gibt ihr die bannende Macht dieses furchtlosen und hoffnungslosen Blickes die Weihe der Form; die Sinnlosigkeit wird, als Sinnlosigkeit, zur Gestalt: sie ist ewig geworden, von der Form bejaht, aufgehoben, und erlöst.)[1]

From the point of view of the Novelle in general, this is doubtless an exaggerated formulation of the element of the irrational and fortuitous that is frequently present in it. But Lukács' ideas are borne out by Stifter's story, both in its style and in its underlying philosophy.

Abdias conforms to other, more traditional criteria of the Novelle also. It has a "Wendepunkt" in the hero's setting out (exactly midway in the narrative) on his hejira to Europe. It has a "Falke" in the lightning which symbolizes the mysterious power of Fate that dominates the action. It has various "Leitmotive." Its "Idee," compressible in brief summary, is furnished by the author's own introductory remarks. There is no "Rahmen" of an organic sort, to be sure, only a moralizing introduction and at the end a mere colophon: "so endeth the tale of the Jew Abdias." But it deals, as the Novelle likes to do, with "das Unerhörte," an extraordinary case of human experience and misfortune. Hence it stands out among the writings of an author who has been called "the genius of the ordinary" because of his deep-set conviction of the value of the small and unpretentious things of everyday life. In its exotic background, too, the African desert with its silence and loneliness, its burning sun and sand, *Abdias* is unique in mood and setting among Stifter's Novellen—for even *Brigitta* has, in the Hungarian *puszta*, a less unfamiliar background.

Abdias tells the hero's story from birth to death, and thus demonstrates anew the capacity of the Novelle to compass an entire lifetime, and one of Faustian length. This is accomplished to some extent by abridgement, as when the fifteen years of Abdias's apprenticeship are summarized in one page. Such condensation does not occur often, however, and is more than outweighed by other pages of dispensable detail. Stifter's addiction to the "little things," his disinclination for the great and the dramatic, though overcome in *Abdias* to a unique degree, are still sufficiently in evidence to impair the slimness and cogency which characterize the Novelle at its best.

A structural feature that makes for economy and cohesion, as well as occasionally for "Stimmung," is the use of leitmotifs. Thus the Roman triumphal arch and the two dessicated palm-trees which mark Abdias's home in the ruins recur repeatedly, as does the tattered aloe by it. Abdias's fine black eyes, and his daughter's blue ones — in fact the color blue, "aus Licht und Nacht gewoben" (102)[2] in sky and sea and distant mountains and in the flax-fields that Ditha loves so well—these are constant factors. From the Bible, which has affected strongly the forms and cadences of Stifter's diction,[3] comes the motif of the angels: Jehovah's Angel of the Pestilence who has disfigured Abdias for life, the "sad, dark Angel" who hovers over his head during his journey and leaves him only when his misfortune is about to be revealed, and the "shining Angel" who hovers over a happier expedition (19, 22, 23, 67). The motif of loneliness, "Ein-

samkeit," has a mood value as well as a characterizing value for
Abdias: it is his lot all through life, the spirit of the African
wastes that he carries with him wherever he goes. As he disembarks in Europe, his infant in his arms, with his servant and
his ass, there lies on all three figures "the grey of the desert and
of far distances" (71). He finds himself a remote, uninhabited
valley over which hangs "a benign charm of solitude and quietness" (71), and remains alone there to the end of his days, for
"he had brought the African spirit and the nature of solitude to
Europe with him" (106).—The most emphatic leitmotif of all,
which recurs with fateful force from the first page to the last,
is that of the lightning. It figures even in a curious image of the
desert battle, where the hero is said to immerse himself in the
lightning of sword-blades, "die Brust gleichsam in Säbelblitze
tauchend" (21).

The account of Ditha's last moments shows a distinctly musical reiteration of the simple and solemn note of death. Ditha
has been speaking of the beauty and wonder of the flax plant
and its role in human life from the cradle to the grave: "und
wenn wir tot sind . . . " She falls silent, and her father, glancing sideways, sees the soft lambent flame that has just "kissed
the life from her head:" "und Ditha lehnte gegen eine Garbe
zurück und war tot." Without uttering a sound, Abdias stares at
this new "thing" beside him, not believing it his daughter. Then
he shakes her and speaks to her, but without avail: "sie sank aus
seiner Hand und war tot" (113). Three times in half a page
this old and awful word resounds, like the tolling of a funeral
bell, or like the sombre triad that opens Beethoven's Fifth Symphony.

The structure of *Abdias* is unusual for a Novelle. It is divided into three unequal parts. Abdias dominates the entire
story that is named for him, but his life consists of three chapters which are dominated by and named for three women who
succeed each other virtually without overlapping: his mother
Esther, his wife Deborah, and his daughter Ditha. The length of
these chapters, the importance of the experience they contain,
the individuation and depth of the women and their spiritual
closeness to Abdias, increase rapidly: the wife is given almost
twice as much space as the mother, the daughter three times as
much as the wife. In Esther we see the doting mother, to whom
Abdias is always her pretty little boy; in Deborah the undiscern-

ing and sterile wife—though the boons withheld are granted in one last brief, tragic moment; in Ditha the child and comrade of his soul, an extension, superficially incredible but symbolically convincing, of the radiant spirit lodged in the repellent body of this paradoxical representative of humanity. Ditha's effect on Abdias's life is the deepest. She is the only one who, with the eyes of the soul, sees the beauty of her father's heart and not the ugliness of his face. With her death, Abdias's life is mentally over, though he lives on physically for thirty long years more.

Though he matures and deepens under affliction, Abdias does not become a saint, as one might say Grillparzer's poor fiddler and Otto Ludwig's Apollonius do. He remains, more like Faust, a dogged, unregenerate specimen of humanity. He fights fate to the last, to that final blow that unhinges his mind. He never accepts his lot in religious humility; this is one thing that distinguishes him from Job, with whom he might in some other respects be compared. Abdias has serious faults. He is as spiritually blind as the girl he marries. Of Deborah it is written that she had only eyes of the body, "leibliche Augen," to see external beauty, not spiritual vision to discern beauty of the heart. But Abdias too saw in her, when they met, nothing but her exceptional beauty, and remembered and married her only for that (18). He has therefore no right to complain when, his beauty being gone, she turns away from him. And in fact he does not complain, nor turn away from her; he is a man of one love, and he holds his marriage sacred.

He has his moments of "hybris," as when he weighs a plan to kill the Bey, become Bey and Sultan himself and conquer and subjugate the whole world (22). His arrogant treatment of Melek comes home to him later, very much as does Meister Anton's treatment of the constable in Hebbel's play. This over-assertion of himself in his outside relations, however, is "compensation" for his lack of recognition and love at home, "denn in der Fremde wurde ihm zuteil, was man ihm zu Hause entzog: Hochachtung, Ansehen, Oberherrschaft" (19-20). His splendor in dress and equipment, which draws upon him and his neighbors Melek's pillaging raid, is likewise compensatory, "denn seit er hässlich war, liebte er den Glanz noch mehr" (20). Once his fighting passions are aroused, Abdias turns forth that "tigerartige Anlage" which Stifter sees in all men.[4]

But with all his faults, Abdias is "ein guter Mensch" in the sense of Goethe's *Prologue in Heaven.* He is just, dutiful, conscientious, even religious and tender. He is kind to his servants, even when they hate and cheat him. He is long-suffering under the abuse of his neighbors. He is kind to animals, and when by an ironical twist of fate he has killed his dog, he is on the point of killing himself in his despair (89). He is utterly devoted to his child, not only in her infancy but later, when her blindness calls forth every resource of his tenderness and pedagogical patience. Repeatedly he thanks Jehovah for the love that has thus been brought into his heart: "dass er einen solchen Strom sanften Fühlens in das Herz des Menschen zu leiten vermöge" (52). Even the passionate thought of revenge on Melek pales before his devotion to Ditha: as they sail from Africa, Abdias descries Melek's white house on the receding shore, but all this world falls astern "wie ein törichtes Märchen" as he turns away and loses himself in gazing upon his child (69).

And yet this man, who in some ways shows human nature at its best, is the very paragon of human misfortune. In the three chapters of his life, the impact of Fate and its inscrutableness increases steadily. The more fully developed the individual, the more shining a mark for Fate. In the earlier calamities we still see some of the ennobling effect which Schiller ascribed to the power that elevated man even as it crushed him: "das grosse, gigantische Schicksal, / Welches den Menschen erhebt, wenn es den Menschen zermalmt."[5] But its ultimate senselessness is underlined by the fact that its final blow deprives Abdias of his reason and hence precludes any further spiritual growth.

Early in the story it is said of the hero: "Abdias ... tat den Tieren, den Sklaven und den Nachbarn Gutes. Aber sie hassten ihn dafür" (18). This is even before he falls victim to the pox in Odessa and suffers the disfigurement (an intensification of Stifter's own) that chiefly turns men's hearts against him; for his experience is a demonstration of the superficiality of men's judgment as well as of the incomprehensibleness of men's fate. His maidservant Mirtha hates him, considering him the murderer of his wife. He is likewise blamed for Ditha's blindness. His servants, though fellow-Jews, dislike and defraud him. When in his age he takes up trading again, in order to provide for his blind child after his death, he becomes "an object of hatred and loathing" (85-86) because of his avarice (Geiz); but years later, when all "Geiz" has vanished and he is a changed man, people still hate him and, with no deeper reason, love his fair daughter at sight (99)—judging as superficially as the woman in the African port who would not go with him to nurse his child (68).

His misfortune with his dog, of whom he was exceedingly fond, draws from the author a comment on the fateful perversity of things in this man's life: "als wenn es mit dem Manne immer hätte so sein müssen, dass sich die Dinge zu den seltensten Widrigkeiten verketteten" (87). A little later, Stifter again comments editorially on "eine jener Wendungen in dem Geschicke dieses Mannes" (90), this time a benevolent turn of fortune, but an equally incomprehensible one: the lightning that gives Ditha sight.

She, like her father, is a "marked" individual, singled out from "gewöhnliche Menschen" in striking ways. Like Abdias in his youth, she has an affinity for lightning, loves thunderstorms, and is a natural conductor of electricity (100). Moreover, as a result of having lived so long in darkness and being brought up in solitude, her evaluation of day and night, of outer and inner life, is the reverse of the ordinary, so that dream and reality merge in her consciousness, and she stands among people with all the strangeness of a humanized flower (101-102).

Ditha's affinity with the lightning expresses in a heightened symbol the enigmatical linking of the things we love best with an inscrutable power that gives them and takes them away. There is something mysterious about Ditha; she appears leagued with natural forces far beyond human ken and control. She seems Nature's child, and at the end Nature reclaims her just as she has reached her flowering.[6] Between Ditha and her father there is something of the same close and fateful relation as between Gnade and Thomas in Meyer's *Der Heilige;* both come with their fathers out of an exotic Oriental background and, "eben aufgeblüht," meet a dreadful fate in a Western land, and the death of each is a blow from which the father never recovers.[7]

There is a special irony in the fate that pursues Ditha. Aware of her "conductivity," Abdias has secured his house with lightning-rods. But her destiny overtakes her in the open; the lightning seems to reach out for her far in advance of the storm itself, stealthily, soft-handed, using only a fraction of its mighty force, for Abdias, himself "conductive," sitting beside her, feels not the slightest tremor, and the landscape remains serene (113). Ironically, the thunderstorm that benevolently gave Ditha sight wrought destruction on Abdias's house and his neighbors' crops (93), while the thunderstorm that takes Ditha's life pours out rich benefaction on all other creatures (114); and each storm is followed by a beautiful rainbow in the east (93-94, 114). These two events illustrate Stifter's introductory observation on the appalling unconcern of Nature: "Heute kommt mit derselben holden Miene Segen, und morgen geschieht das Entsetzliche" (5).

Stifter was acutely aware of the immense and unsolved problem raised by his story, for he prefaced it with several pages of meditation on Fate, Nature, and human destiny. He distinguishes between the "fatum" of the ancients—conceived as the final, unyielding substratum of all happening, the ultimate irrationality of being—and the milder modern concept of "Schicksal" as something sent upon us (which at least implies a sender, a supreme Mind). But there is, he tells himself, a third possibility: that all that happens is part of an endless chain of causes and effects, laws of Nature which we now but dimly discern, but which some day, with increase of reason and insight, we shall recognize as an unbroken garland of flowers (heitre Blumenkette) hanging down through eternity to a Hand that holds its end. In that future time there will be no more chance, only consequences; no more misfortune, but only the logical results of wrong-doing; for it is only the gaps in our present knowledge that cause our bafflement, and our misconduct that results in unhappiness (5-6).[8]

All this sounds like the logical optimism of a typical eighteenth-century Rationalist. But if we look more closely, we find neither the logic nor the optimism wholly convincing. Even syntactically, it is disconcerting to see Stifter (6) slide from a tentative statement (eigentlich mag es . . .) to an "indicative condition" (haben wir dereinstens recht gezählt, und können wir . . . dann wird . . .) and from that to an unconditional asseveration (denn die Lücken . . . erzeugen . . .). Thus what began as a conjecture ends seemingly as an established fact.

Stifter is a poor logician and metaphysician, but a first-rate story-teller, and it is a true instinct that makes him turn away from such fruitless speculation (Wir wollen nicht weiter grübeln . . . 7) to tell the story of a man whose career disproves at every turn the facile optimism we have just heard expounded, and makes the "heitre Blumenkette" seem a paltry garland incapable of concealing the steely cable of Necessity beneath. Optimism about life may be Stifter's wish, but pessimism is his conviction, a pessimism that was in the air in a period when men still recalled the fateful years of Napoleon and still labored under the reactionary rule of Metternich, while lending their ears to the "Weltschmerz" of Byron and Lenau and the disheartening philosophy of Schopenhauer.

In *Abdias* Stifter does not reach a solution of the problem of Fate, for we see him wrestling with it again in *Der Hochwald*. Indeed, at the end of the philosophical "aside" in *Abdias* he admits that his hero's career is one of those that make one ask "why this?" and plunge one into gloomy brooding about Providence, Destiny, and the ultimate basis of all things (7). And, artist that he is—not philosopher nor theologian—Stifter, as he begins his tale, asks us neither to curse nor bless, but only to contemplate attentively the "Bild," the picture of a man that he will put before us (7).

This picture is drawn with a remarkable realism, a realism that is all Stifter's own, that is neither "poetic" nor "dramatic" in intent, for it does not consciously select nor enhance nor intensify, but results from a loving, catholic concern for all the ordinary, small, "insignificant" things of life. This style is in a sense the purest "naturalism," for it reflects Nature with complete impartiality, convinced that there is in it neither "great" nor "small."[9] It is unsentimental, as Nature is; it avoids, instead of seeking, pathos and tragedy. One might say that Stifter's view, consistently maintained, would make tragedy impossible. There is in his "nature-mindedness" a limitation that he shares with Goethe. Where the dramatic (and the Romantic) mind "dramatizes," sees beginnings and catastrophic endings, Stifter sees, or tries to see, only the even operation of Nature's timeless law. He is a uniquely epic writer, not a dramatizer but a story-teller, with something of the broad and unhurried impartiality or "Wahllosigkeit" of Nature herself. Anyone with a taste for drama who reads Stifter's long novels, for instance *Witiko*, is disappointed time and again by Stifter's inability or unwillingness to realize dramatic possibilities inherent in his situations (one has a similar experience, say, with Goethe's *Egmont*). In *Abdias*, for example, a feeling of anti-climax results when, after all the elaborate preparations for danger, the long desert journey passes without event: "Aber es traf keine der gefürchteten Gefahren ein" (66).

There is a religious spirit in Stifter's love and respect for things, even the commonest ones, as exponents of the mysterious, still uncomprehended laws underlying all life. In a pebble is locked up the secret of the universe; the smallest grain of sand is a wonder: "Es ist das kleinste Sandkörnlein ein Wunder, dessen *Wesenheit* man nicht ergründen kann."[10] One is reminded of William Blake's line about seeing the world in a grain of sand. This sense of wonder and reverence for the small, "Andacht zum Kleinen," might also be claimed as Romantic qualities in Stifter.

In the Preface to his *Bunte Steine*, Stifter defended himself against the charge that he dealt only with small things and ordinary people. But what is "gross," he asks. Great, for him, are the quiet things of Nature: the breeze, the murmuring brook, the growing grain. The tempest, the earthquake are not greater, but in fact smaller, for in all their violence they are but limited and transient manifestations of the great laws. There is the same force in milk that boils over on the kitchen stove as in the volcano's eruption. The savage is overwhelmed by individual cataclysms; the enlightened modern man is aware of the great principles behind them. And so it is with human nature: the sum of a simple, industrious, reasonable, faithful lifetime is greater than big, passionate crises.

One hears in all this not only the voice of religious humility and love, or of Goethe's "Natursinn" consistently developed, but also the voice of the narrower 18th-century Rationalism or the muted note of the Austrian "Biedermeier." The Biedermeier "Bescheidenheit" is found also in Grillparzer. But it is far from being the whole of Grillparzer. And Grillparzer was a born dramatist, while Stifter's bent was anti-dramatic—though on occasion, as in *Abdias*, his art belies his philosophy. One could readily reduce his theories to an absurdity by pointing out that, with their logical application, Voss's *Luise* would count as a greater work of literature than *Othello* or *Penthesilea*.

But there is a grandeur in this natural simplicity, nevertheless. In *Abdias* as in other works Stifter deals with Man and Nature, Man in Nature, not the master of it but subordinated to it and its great ways. Abdias is shown always closely tied to the earth, to natural necessities, to sun and sand and water and the countless daily adjustments to them. Ditha is even more deeply bound to Nature, immediate and remote, to flowers and lightning. She develops naturally, unhurriedly, like a "speaking flower" (102). An act of Nature gives her sight, another takes her away in her prime. Her musing upon the connection between a plant and human life prepares gently and imperceptibly for her death and mitigates its catastrophic suddenness. We feel vaguely that this brief life has fulfilled itself according to some dimly descried natural necessity, and we are filled with awe rather than poignant grief. She is taken up into Nature's unending processes; from her fair and unpolluted flesh new flowers spring: "aus Dithas Gliedern sprossten Blumen und Gras," says Stifter (114), with perhaps an unconscious reminiscence of the "bluomen unde gras" of his great compatriot Walther. Abdias, by contrast, is left standing like a mighty tree, battered by storms, riven and blanched by one final lightning-bolt, to fall at last from sheer decay, simply and without drama: "Eines Tages sass er nicht mehr dort, die Sonne schien auf den leeren Platz" (114). And from his grave, too, the grasses grow.

This patient and all-embracing nature-mindedness of Stifter's leads to a wealth of detail in *Abdias* that is dispensable and even undesirable in the Novelle as such. We get a full description of the desert ruins and the mode of life in them; we get a complete itemization of Abdias's preparations for the trip through the desert, and its course. We get a long account of Ditha's development, her blindness, and the father's methods of dealing with it and its after-effects; here, one feels, the pedagogue Stifter has displaced the poet. Domestic animals are named and individualized. We are even told, with pedantic particularity, how Abdias waters Kola, the she-ass, partly from the cistern above ground and partly from the cooler cistern under the house (51).

And yet, although we are shown, it seems to us, Abdias's every act and movement to the smallest detail, we are told virtually nothing of what goes on within him. Once, indeed, as he sits by his dead wife and weeps tears "like molten bronze" (38), we get a glimpse of his thoughts that go back to his first meeting with Deborah. But in scene after scene his inner reactions remain hidden, as he "says nothing" or "falls silent" or "walks away." There are no soliloquies, no such careful analyses of the psychological concomitants of outward action as those elaborated by Ludwig in *Zwischen Himmel und Erde*. We are left to imagine the inward drama and to decide for ourselves the question about the hero which the author expressly leaves open: whether his fate or his character is the greater enigma (ob sein Schicksal ein seltsameres Ding sei, oder sein Herz, 7).

This Novelle would sag sadly under its weight of detail, were it not for the admirable cogency and terseness which Stifter commands in the crucial scenes. The same matter-of-fact realism that can linger over the accoutrements of the she-ass can show with unceremonious brevity Abdias's beautiful mother become an aged scold, his father feeble-minded, both of them childish and of no further account (17). The persons in the story are never idealized and are treated without sentimentality. Any incipient pathos is checked by some sober observation. Thus Abdias kisses Deborah's cheek in a last farewell, and notes "sie war jetzt schon kalt." In the flickering candlelight, he can fancy she still breathes; "aber es atmete nichts, und das Starren der toten Glieder dauerte fort. Auch das Kind regte sich nicht. Als sei es gleichfalls gestorben." The very sentences have the dull finality of the fact of death. A moment later, Abdias looks wistfully into the infant's face to detect a likeness with its mother; "aber," Stifter explains soberly, "er entdeckte sie nicht, denn das Kind war noch zu klein" (39). Of the women who appear to prepare Deborah's body for burial, Stifter observes caustically that some had come to lament, "as was their business," others to get a thrill out of the sad affair, and still others merely to gaze (40). The immediately following passage is an unsparing analysis of the hysterical behavior of the servant-girl Mirtha.

Stifter's realism at times comes close to what was later to be called Naturalism. Thus we see Abdias, coming home across the desert on foot, carrying in his hand a piece of a horse's cadaver, from which he tears off bits to throw to the jackals (14). We are told about the preparation of Deborah's body, including the detail that the corpse, not yet rigid, grows relaxed in the warm water and lets its naked limbs hang (41). So at the end we are shown the dead Ditha's head and arm dangling over her father's shoulder (113). Stifter does not hesitate to liken the grass filling that pours from torn pillows to the extruded entrails of a human body (43).

If such comparisons point forward to Naturalism, there are others that point backward to Romanticism, like the figure of Abdias's throwing his wild Bedouin thoughts like Atlas vultures against Ditha's heart (107). Ditha's pronounced synaesthesia takes us back to the world of Hoffmann. She speaks of "penetrating sounds (bohrende Klänge) which had been there, cutting, dumb, or upright notes that had been standing in the room" (93). When she first sees a field of blossoming flax, she exclaims: "Father, look! The whole heaven is ringing (klingt) on the tips of these green upright filaments!" (102). She also experiences "violet" sounds, which she likes better than "those that stand erect and are unpleasant, like glowing rods" (102).

There is a pictorial and picturesque quality of "Stimmung" in Stifter's style, as there is in Keller's, that links them both, as writers and as painters, with Romanticism. The brief passage on the opening page—the white-robed Bedouin riding under a darkened sky over the yellow sand of his desert, suddenly struck down by a flash of lightning—makes a painting that could serve as a frontispiece to *Abdias*, for it combines essential motifs of the story in a vision born of Stifter's pictorial imagination. The scenes in the devastated room, lit fitfully by a candle, in which Deborah has just died, show the hand of the painter in the use of lights and shadows and colors. We see the black slave-boy Uram, "like a statue cast of dark bronze," crouching motionless on the earth floor beside the waxen-pale body of his mistress (37). We see Abdias's long shadow falling across the dead woman as he stoops over his child (39). We are shown Abdias disembarking with the baby and Uram and the ass—an outlandish trio such as the European port has not seen in many days, a striking study in figures and colors.

In the large canvas of the battle-scene, our eye is drawn to such details as Abdias's haggard, dark-skinned arm, outstretched in command, contrasting with the silken sleeve that falls back from it (21). The contrast in types and colors as the "black"-faced, white-haired, decrepit old Abdias walks beside his beautiful, golden-haired young daughter must have delighted the painter's eye (99). The final scene has, besides its repeated sound-motifs of lark-song and distant thunder, marked chromatic qualities: the blue-and-green flax field, the yellow grain in stubble and sheaves, the deep-blue sky gradually overrun with storm-clouds; and, a few moments later, the gaunt, Lear-like figure of Abdias, his dead child in his arms, his white hair waving in the wind, striding down through the grainfield—the very picture of Tragic Man (111, 113).

In addition to these more distinctly pictorial scenes there are others full of dramatic action. The most impressive is that of the battle with the Bedouin raiders in the desert (20-22): the attack, the timidity of the caravan people, and Abdias's taking command as the natural leader; his dark face uplifted, its scars flaming like fire, its eyes like white stars, his commands in deep, sonorous Arabic rolling over the battlefield—this is a picture which combines the Homeric and the Romantic-exotic, a triumph of the imagination unaided by experience. Vivid details of the fighting, the cruel massacre of the surrendering foe by those who had themselves but lately pleaded for mercy, the plundering of the bodies, the concluding vignette of the Turk who obsequiously wipes Abdias's bloody blade on his own caftan—all this is the demonstration of a realism of violent action that is as amazing as it is rare in Stifter's work.

Equally impressive in their way are the brief, vivid dialogue-scenes: Abdias and the slave-boy Uram (30f.), Abdias negotiating with the hostile neighbors (33-35). There is an austere pathos in the last scene of Deborah's life: the childbirth in utter forsakenness, on the naked earth, bereft of all comforts and aid, and yet her uncomplaining patience, her new tenderness for Abdias that brings the pair, so long estranged, together again for one tragically brief moment (27-28). The pathos, however, is engendered only in us; Stifter does not point to it nor join in it; it is strictly our own reaction to what he presents with impersonal objectivity. His words, like those of old Anna Margaret in Brentano's story, are "even and cold" (gleichmässig und kalt), deeply affecting even when they tersely record the horrible. He speaks, as it were, through the rigid mask of antique tragedy, with a "placid innocence" (gelassene Unschuld) like that of the inhuman laws of Nature (5). Thus Deborah's death is reported in a detached, understated, even ironical way: "Aber sie hatte einer Pflege nicht mehr not; denn da er ausser Hause war, hatte sie nicht geschlummert, sondern sie war gestorben" (36). The same unemotional chronicling covers Abdias's feelings: "Am andern Tage begrub Abdias sein Weib in dem steinernen Grabe und zahlte die zwei versprochenen Goldstücke" (42). Then Deborah's epitaph is pronounced in the simple words: "Sie hatte wenig Glück in dieser Ehe gehabt, und als es angefangen hätte, musste sie sterben" (42).

The same ironic laconism prevails in the report of Ditha's death, years later (113). Seeing the faint light over her head, Abdias thinks "sie habe wieder ihren Schimmer" (her customary electric reaction during thunderstorms). "Aber sie hatte ihren Schimmer nicht gehabt," continues Stifter dryly. "Da er hinblickte, war schon alles vorüber. Es war auf den Schein ein kurzes, heiseres Krachen gefolgt, und Ditha lehnte gegen eine Garbe zurück und war tot." As a sort of "buffer" against our emotion, Stifter immediately turns our attention to Nature: "Kein Tropfen Regen fiel, nur die dünnen Wolken rieselten, wie schnell gezogene Schleier, über den Himmel." Then we observe Abdias—his movements only: "Der Greis gab nicht einen Laut von sich, . . . er starrte . . . er schüttelte sie . . . Dann stand der Mann auf, lud das tote Mädchen mechanisch auf seine Schulter und trug sie nach Hause." The grim "mechanisch" seems like a fatalistic summing-up of Abdias's battered life. This is not even Abdias and Ditha any more, but a "Greis," a "Mann," a "Mädchen" reduced to basic human terms. Language here reaches the lapidary style of primitive sculpture. Equally elementary and stark is that earlier scene in which Abdias attends Deborah in her extremity. Here we have humanity in its simplest aspect: a man, a woman, and their newborn child together on the hard earth—it might be in some prehistoric cave, even before the advent of articulate speech, for here words are not needed and are hardly used.

For all its wealth of realistic detail, we cannot assign *Abdias* to any particular period. There are no references to contemporary history to date it. Much of it seems to move in the patriarchal world of the Old Testament; but then again there are much more modern touches: we frequently see firearms (there are even four-barrelled pistols), and we hear of "English papers," evidently drafts or banknotes. The story opens in the ruins of "eine alte, aus der Geschichte verlorene Römerstadt" deep in the sandy wastes of the Atlas range in North Africa—a place as it were withdrawn from time and plunged into anonymity. It lost its name centuries ago, it is not marked on any map, it is the refuge only of jackals and of a scattered remnant of that race which in its dispersion and in its toughness under adversity could well have been taken as a symbol for the ancient and indestructible human race itself.

Though Abdias is formally entitled "der Jude Abdias" at the beginning and at the end, he is not a typical representative of the Jewish or of any other race. It is significant that on his journey home with his bride he passes for an armed Turk (16), and at the close of the desert battle he is treated as a triumphant Emir (22). During the fight, and in his later years with Ditha, he speaks Arabic. He sets forth into life, to be sure, from an Old Testament setting, a young trader out for gain. But as he roams the earth for fifteen years, with the wind and rain of many lands in his face and the many tongues of mankind in his ear, he seems to become the symbol for Man as such, struggling for survival in the teeming sea of his kind, accommodating himself to ever new necessities, rising undaunted under the blows of fate to prove that man's permanence is not in his works but in his spirit.

It is characteristic of Abdias that always "fing er etwas anderes an" (103). As an old man, not unlike Faust, he undertakes to reclaim an allegedly sterile valley; he becomes a large-scale farmer, employing a great band of laborers drawn from distant parts (103). Like Faust, he is no saint; he is still capable of vindictive passion; "er wollte jetzt nach Afrika reisen, um Melek ein Messer in das Herz zu stossen" (114); but he has grown too feeble for this. Yet as long as his mind holds he continues to act and to plan. This is the spirit of humanity, ever-endangered, ever-insecure, but ever-creating. This is the invincible vitality that in Goethe's great *Prologue* drives the demon of destruction to despair. By the end of his long life (he is said to have been well over 100), Abdias has taken on the heroic proportions of legend, and we feel his death less as the decease of an individual than as the transmutation of an indestructible vital force.

CHAPTER SIX
GRILLPARZER, *DER ARME SPIELMANN* (1848)

Franz Grillparzer was, like Kleist, primarily a dramatist, and he had no very high regard for his two narrative works, the somewhat sensational *Kloster bei Sendomir* and the much finer *Spielmann*. He regarded stories as not being his "field" in any case, and refused requests to write any others.[1] The *Spielmann* he designated as a "simple and unpretentious tale,"[2] deprecating the name "Novelle" for it when he sent it to the publisher.[3] Heyse, however, who was surely a judge in such matters, regarded it as an exemplary Novelle, indeed prized it as the one that had first inspired him to make his famous collection, the *Novellenschatz*.[4] Nevertheless, Grillparzer seems to have felt that, in comparison with the classical standards of Goethe and Cervantes, not to say Kleist, his story did not deserve to be called a Novelle—and indeed his earlier tale, *Das Kloster bei Sendomir*, more readily satisfies the formal requirements of this genre,[5] whereas the *Spielmann* constitutes a deepening and hence a "violation" of it, as we shall see.

Yet one can say that *Der arme Spielmann* displays all the essential earmarks of a Novelle as set forth by earlier and contemporary theorists: it has a "frame"—and a very interesting and novel one—a "turning-point" (the crisis in the family's fortunes and the death of Jakob's father, midway in the "inner" story); it focuses attention on two central figures of established character; it has a "falcon" in Jakob's violin and a leitmotif in Barbara's song; and it could, at need, be summarized in one sentence.

But Grillparzer may be said to have enlarged the scope of the Novelle by making it the vehicle of objectified self-revelation. He also deepened it as a vessel of psychological revelation in general, and thus adapted it to more modern uses. For here the factor of event (Begebenheit or Ereignis) is reduced to a minimum and is subordinated to the exhibition of character. There is no "drama" here of the kind in Kleist's *Kohlhaas*; the hero has no opponent to fight. In fact, the hero is no "hero," but one of those obscure existences that stand at the lower end of the scale from the demigods of literature—and yet are psychologically of a piece with them, as the author tells us in one of the most significant *ex cathedra* passages in the "frame:" "Truly, one cannot comprehend the famous unless one has emotionally relived the obscure. From the wrangling of wine-flushed barrow-pushers to the contentions of the gods there runs an invisible but unbroken thread; and in the young serving-maid who, half against her will, follows her importunate lover away from the throng of the dancers, there lie in embryo all your Juliets, Didos, and Medeas" (Wahrlich! man kann die Berühmten nicht verstehen, wenn man die Obskuren nicht durchgefühlt hat. Von dem Wortwechsel weinerhitzter Karrenschieber spinnt sich ein unsichtbarer aber ununterbrochener Faden bis zum Zwist der Göttersöhne, und in der jungen Magd, die, halb wider Willen, dem drängenden Liebhaber seitab vom Gewühl der Tanzenden folgt, liegen als Embryo die Julien, die Didos und die Medeen, 39).[6]

This "psychological" bias was to become more and more characteristic of the modern Novelle. The next great example of it is Mörike's *Mozart auf der Reise nach Prag*. There, to be sure, we have a "hero" and a great musician, not a would-be one; yet the emphasis is not on the heroic but on the human and on the unfathomable mystery of genius. The "central event" is of no greater moment than the picking of an orange, and all that happens is instrumental to the exhibition of a unique personality. The same attenuation of outward incident marks the psychological Novelle of the 20th century, for example Mann's *Tonio Kröger*.

Der arme Spielmann, like the *Judenbuche* and like the later *Schimmelreiter*, comprehends a whole lifetime, and this is another departure from the traditional canon of the Novelle. But whereas Annette von Droste-Hülshoff achieves this condensation, even more concisely than does Storm, by means of a cinema-like spotlighting of crucial scenes in chronological order, Grillparzer employs a technique like that of Meyer's lapidary epic *Huttens letzte Tage:* from near the end of the hero's life, as through a window, we gain a retrospective view of his previous career. Such procedure also entails a factor of selection, as memory sifts the matter of experience, and this selectivity is quite in keeping with the Novelle ideal. Grillparzer's procedure is, moreover, essentially similar to that of the "analytic" drama: he starts in just before the final catastrophe and, by progressively unrolling a past action while advancing a present one, he gives to his simple tale an uncommon depth and tension.

The story has actually a double "frame" and two narrators, both of whom, as will appear, represent Grillparzer. A Viennese gentleman and author interested in types of humanity observes a "Volksfest" and encounters there a fiddler whose extraordinary appearance and manner fascinate him. He visits him later in his attic room and hears his story from his own lips. The narrator tells us what the hero tells him, and supplements it with facts and observations which only he could have supplied, especially at the close, after the hero's death. We are thus twice removed from the actual "Begebenheit" as given directly, say, in Kleist's unframed Novellen. The frame with its interruptions and retardations, its seemingly chance encounters and re-encounters, adds to the impression of "true-life" objectivity, and never strikes us as a literary contrivance for the exhibition of the author's self and "other" self. In Grillparzer's hands the Novelle proves that capacity for objectified subjectivity and even irony that Friedrich Schlegel had attributed to it.

The initial part of the frame is broad, four times as broad as the final one: the story, including much of the hero's as well as the narrator's, present life, has run almost one-third its length before the "inner" story, told by the hero about his past, begins. At the end of that, and within a few pages of the end of the whole, we return to the hero's present, or rather we hear, with the narrator, of the manner of the hero's death. The hero had thrice briefly interrupted his story (reverting to the "frame" present), and there is a longer interim (a trip of the narrator's) before the brief epilogue.

Despite this arithmetical discrepancy, the two frames give the impression of complete balance, and this impression is strengthened by a symmetrical correspondence of motifs, first and last.[7] The public festival of the opening is balanced by the public calamity of the close, the flood of holiday folk at the beginning (a figure carried through at some length) by the flood of destructive waters at the end; a gateway in the park with the joyous living, a gateway in the flooded suburb with the bodies of the dead. Each flood casts its derelicts ashore: the wretched little company of "Volksmusikanten" at the edge of the park road, and the corpses of the drowned awaiting the coroner. In other, less striking instances, also, this antiphonal balance of motifs is observable.

The broader opening frame gives us a good deal of information about the narrator: his views on the common people and the critics, his habits and daily routine—"asides" which are quite dispensable for a Novelle of any other but this self-revealing psychological type. For the old fiddler's interlocutor is Grillparzer himself, as the one in *Kasperl und Annerl* was Brentano himself. Here we can glimpse the author at his creative work, weaving this very story as he sits in the deserted "Wirtsgarten" or walks pensively homeward.[8]

The double frame (which is double at each end) and the two narrators, "outer" and "inner", make possible a novel and subtle interrelation between author, story, and reader. Jakob, the old fiddler, has both subjective and objective value: he is a part of Grillparzer and yet an independent literary creation. He is the author's darling (Liebling), yet is drawn with a certain detachment and even irony. As he looks back upon his own youth and tells the tale of his lost love, he induces an elegiac mood not unlike that in Storm's *Immensee*. On the other hand the "outer" narrator, the Viennese gentleman, provides an objective and present view of Jakob by an onlooker and also reports the estimation of Jakob by his neighbors and the public at large. In his own guileless account, he appears to us as a rare, saintly spirit; in the eyes of his practical fellows, as a "queer duck" and a failure. Thus light is cast on the hero (and to a lesser extent on other characters)[9] from two sides, and this greatly enhances the "relief" of the portraiture.

Such plasticity is, of course, the mark of a great dramatist. Though Grillparzer is present in both the hero and the narrator, he maintains the dramatist's impartial objectivity. He offers no "leading" comment or sentimental interpretation, but simply presents, on a stage within a stage, figures speaking and acting, and leaves us to draw our own conclusions and feel our own feelings. He avoids easy opportunities to "dramatize," but even as a story-teller he is still, like Kleist, a master of the theater. Even incidental personages are distinctly outlined, for example, the "Spielleute" in the park who lead up to the first introduction of Jakob. Him we see with phenomenal lifelikeness from first to last. Never has a character with such personal implications been more impersonally represented. How vividly we see him in his room, taking his visitor's hat and laying it on the bed, crossing his legs in an easy posture, picking some lint from his threadbare trousers, propping his chin in his hand and tilting his head sideways as he seems to look down the vistas of memory in beginning his story (50-51). How eloquent is his self-depreciatory gesture "mit auseinanderfallenden Händen" as he casts his eyes over his unimpressive figure—"but she wouldn't have wanted me" (74). Incidentally, movements of the hands are most effectively used throughout.

The other leading actor, Barbara, is likewise introduced in characteristic attitude and gestures and speech — fully and impressively individuated in her first few moments "on stage" (57-58). How subtle a touch is her little feminine movement in smoothing the hair over her ears as she hears of Jakob's family connections (62)—and, in drastic contrast thereto, her father's comic facial reaction to the same disclosure! Her farewell visit to Jakob's room is a fully acted-out scene (74-75). And so one could go on pointing out dramatic qualities in a story that is instinct with vivifying movement and gesture.

For all its deep emotional issues, *Der arme Spielmann* is marked by objective, unsentimental realism. There is nothing here of the false "romantic" picture of the Vienna of gaiety and music and gracious idleness which the "movies" of our own curiously sentimental age have fabricated. Grillparzer knew his "Alt-Wien" and its workaday reality as few men did, and for all his kinship with Romanticism he did not romanticize it. He saw its "wretched huts" (46), its inequities of class and privilege—"Standesunterschied" is apparent throughout—its slum sections where in a flood the poor, caught in their low-lying huts, drowned like rats in a trap. Even the folk-festival at the beginning has a sombre undertone: this one day of unsophisticated delights is but a momentary interlude in the toilsome and penurious lives of these "Kinder der Dienstbarkeit und der Arbeit" (37).

Aside from the narrator, we meet no one of a higher social class, but we see a whole gallery of the "kleine Leute" and the poor, to whom the hero is attracted early and with whom he comes to be numbered. In Barbara and her father (a worthy pendant to old Miller in Schiller's *Kabale und Liebe*), in her later husband and children, in the customers of the store, in Jakob's neighbors and roommates (the latter through their "setting" alone), we get indelible and unembellished pictures of the plain "Wiener Volk" at their festivity, at a funeral, at home, at work, in the whole round of their humble lives.

This new social consciousness, the concern with "das arbeitende Volk" (37), the recognition of the tragedy and greatness inherent in nameless lives, were by no means absent from Romanticism. One recalls Heine's unfeigned sympathy with the Harz miners and the Silesian weavers, or Chamisso's poems on old beggars and washerwomen, not to mention Brentano's *Kasperl und Annerl*. But a further, more realistic stage of the interest in obscure folk and their tragedies as fit matter for great art is reached in such writers as Droste-Hülshoff and Grillparzer. In the present story, the unvarnished realism in the description of the variously deformed and repulsive beggar-musicians in the park, and in the corpses left by the flood: some piled in courtyards, some still clutched to the grated windows, can be matched only by the closing scene of the *Judenbuche*, and both can be said to anticipate the unsparing Naturalism of a later day.

This external, social realism is paired with an internal, psychological realism. *Der arme Spielmann* is Grillparzer's most "confessional" work, a unique and remarkable fusion of epic outwardness with lyric inwardness. The vivid scenes of "Volksleben" and the hero's share in it are balanced by equally vivid exposition of the deepest recesses of his soul-life. Grillparzer has done here what Goethe was so prone to do: split himself into two halves and let them expound or debate his own personal problems. The narrator, a "Wiener Herr" of higher class, represents Grillparzer on his outer, social side as an evidently successful, distinguished, well-to-do gentleman and author. The fiddler represents Grillparzer's consciousness of his inner, problematical self with all its aspirations and frustrations, its high artistic ideals and its dismal failures—so at least they seemed to him in the critical years when this story was written, years of disillusionment, when fame was fast slipping from his grasp and his hypochondriac self-criticism became intense. The mechanism of "displacement" here is very similar to that in Poe's *The Fall of the House of Usher:* beside the figure who manifestly represents him, the author has placed another, less obviously autobiographical, who impersonates his more questionable self, with psychic depths which he feels reluctant and yet impelled to reveal.[10]

Despite all the other people in the story, it is essentially an inner dialogue, a "Selbstgespräch" objectivated in Grillparzer's naturally dramatic mind. It is not unlike Goethe's *Tasso*, except that the *Spielmann* is recollected in tranquillity; it is a story, after all, not a play, an epic review of past action rather than a dramatization of a present one. But it, no less, is a lament motivated by the urge "zu sagen, wie ich leide"—which was, as Grillparzer confessed, a fundamental urge in his poetic production. He once said that all his works were "Klagen" (Was ihr für Lieder haltet, es sind Klagen); and *Der arme Spielmann* is the most poignant and personal of them all. Yet the fiddler, like Tasso, is not simply equatable with half of the author; in the hands of a great "maker," he grows into a fully rounded figure in his own right, vividly realized in every action and word, invested with unmistakable idiosyncrasies—as impressive an example of character-creation as any in Grillparzer's dramas.

Grillparzer has put so much of himself into this tale that it is virtually a repository for information about his character and convictions. Details of his family life: his stern, rational father, the fate of his brothers, his schooling, his official life versus his real life in private, his personal appearance; his love of order, his sense of privacy, his over-conscientiousness, timidity, and shrinking from life; his withdrawal, failing of public approbation, into the refuge of purely subjective satisfaction in his art; his love of music and improvising, his revelling in the sensuous beauty of mere tones, and his belief that words spoil music; his lack of robust fibre that rendered him unable either to conquer a hostile world or to disdain it; and, most bitter of all, his inability to win the woman he loved.

In his *Selbstbiographie* Grillparzer tells how at one period of his life he delighted himself for half-days at a time playing on an old stringless piano, without feeling the lack of physical sound.[11] This is an even more pronounced subjectivity than that of the fiddler, whose inward ear is enraptured by the beautiful music he produces, while to the listener it is utter cacophony. "Ich möchte eine Tragödie in *Gedanken* schreiben können," said Grillparzer wistfully; "es würde ein Meisterwerk werden!"[12] Other poets, of course, have made similar confessions; thus Kleist admits "dass ich das, was ich mir vorstelle, schön finde, nicht das, was ich leiste."[13] Or Conrad Ferdinand Meyer, questioning the authenticity of his poetic gift, asks himself, in *Möwenflug:* "Gaukelst du im Kreis mit Fabeldingen?/ Oder hast du Blut in deinen Schwingen?"

But no poet that I know of has produced such a sustained and deeply moving embodiment of his self-criticism as this. And from the deepest psychic levels of all comes his depiction of a man's inadequacy in the face of a woman. Jakob kisses Barbara just once—through a glass door. He does not succeed in forcing the door open; it would be contrary to his nature to smash the glass—which was doubtless what Barbara wanted him to do. So in Grillparzer's experience with women there was always a last door which he could not or would not open. He remained always, like Mann's Tonio Kröger, outside the glass, looking in at life's dance. No one can ever say—certainly Grillparzer himself could not have said—how much of the spiritual force that produced his poetic works was a compensation for this deepseated sense of the failure of his sexual life. But no one can fail to hear the lash of the cruelest self-castigation when Grillparzer has Barbara burst out contemptuously: "Ich hasse die weibischen Männer!" (71).

All Grillparzer's major problems: art, woman, faith and inward peace, society—are symbolically represented in *Der arme Spielmann*, even though they are not solved there. His misgivings as to his poetic ability are of course most simply answered by the work itself: this "Klage" over his half-talents, as Kleist called his in a like despair, is itself a supreme proof of his creative genius. He possessed what his hero merely longs for, the power of production. Jakob is only a primitive or potential Grillparzer. He has, in an exaggerated form, Grillparzer's helplessness in dealing with the outside world, while his "inside" world, though rich, never becomes productive. He has the artist's capacity for illusion only to the degree of ludicrous self-deception as to the quality of his performance, never to the degree of creation. His is, like Werther's, the tragedy of the artistic disposition rather than of the artist. In some striking ways he is a forerunner of Mann's Hanno Buddenbrook.

His interlocutor, on the other hand, *is*, we are given to understand, a creative artist, a successful author and dramatist, whose mind we see at work on this "interesting case." There is a sort of nightmarish "Doppelgängertum" here, like that in *Die Judenbuche:* the well-dressed "feiner Herr" condescends to and patronizes his protégé much as Friedrich Mergel did Johannes Niemand. And yet both of them are Grillparzer. It is as though the author had made a caricature of himself and said with a shudder: "There, but for the grace of God, go I." Or as though he had let the successful, inspired half of his consciousness sit in judgment on the unhappy, self-accusing half. The judge tells us nothing of his own successes, but exaggerates the sins and shortcomings of the accused. The mirror-effect of the double frame and double characterization makes possible a bewildering array of reflexes of a very modern sort.

And yet, though he appears as one of life's defeated, the old fiddler is, in a deeper sense, one of life's victors. Though he is the vehicle for some of Grillparzer's severest self-arraignment, he is also a "Wunschbild," an object of longing, for his creator, as Anna Margaret was for Brentano. To Gottfried Keller, Jakob exemplified the power of an absolutely pure soul over the world, "die Gewalt der absolut reinen Seele über die Welt."[14] He illustrates several of the Beatitudes, for he is blessed as are the meek, and the poor in spirit, and the pure in heart. He is deeply religious; he tries to play "den lieben Gott" on his cracked violin, and in the midst of his thwarted and penniless existence he never ceases to be grateful for God's many mercies (55, 70). His very selflessness, which comes close to saintliness, saves him from succumbing to his own bitter troubles; when Barbara marries another man, his first anguish is soon wiped out by the thought that she is now secure, and possessed of the things that he, the "hearth- and homeless one," could never have given her (76). He is utterly naïve and like an animal that refuses to look at itself in a mirror. Only because he does not consider himself important does he escape despair over himself. He does not know brooding upon himself nor self-pity; until interrogated so persistently by his visitor, it had never occurred to him that he had a "story" worth telling (50). And in the spirit of this complete selflessness, he does achieve heroism at the end, even in the conventional sense, for he loses his life in rescue-work during the flood.

Jakob is a strikingly lonely figure: isolated from his fellow-musicians, cast off by his family and class, given up by Barbara, separated by a symbolical chalk-line from his coarse room-mates. Yet he draws from this isolation supreme strength; like a saint, he is in the world but not of it. And, like a saint, he never becomes truly tragic. His armor of selflessness is never pierced; the inmost citadel of his soul, moated with solitude, is never taken. He does not suffer that inner conflict in which Grillparzer's tragic heroes and heroines perish. He is spared the utter breakdown that would have come had he ever realized his complete failure in music. He has built up a defense of unshakeable belief in the beauty of the melody he produces, the depth of his "Kenntnisse" of musical art (77), and the importance of his professional duties (Berufsgeschäfte, 77). When he fails to produce anything like the waltz the children in the street are clamoring for, he insists he *was* playing a waltz, only the children have no ear. When people give him alms out of sheer pity, he accepts them as honoraria for his performance, as he has seen greater virtuosos do (77). When people laugh at him, he endeavors patiently to improve their deplorable taste.

There is no breaking down such defenses. Even his "Entbürgerlichung," his exile from his social class and family, remains more technical than real. For he clings to bourgeois ideals and forms as tenaciously as do the lovers in Keller's *Romeo und Julia*. Meticulously dressed, he plays in the park from a musicstand and notes. The money dropped into his hat is for him an honorable return gift for the gift of aesthetic pleasure he has bestowed on his listeners. Any further donation would be charity, and he strictly refuses it (45). He has become associated with the "public musicians" (öffentliche Musikleute, 44), but he never admits being a "Bettelmusikant." The neatness of his dress and lodging, his well-bred speech and manners, are "standesgemäss" values stoutly maintained.

And thus he has preserved, in his humble career, faith in himself, the integrity of his personality, and the purity of heart which impressed Keller. On the other hand, Grillparzer's favorite preachment of the vanity of greatness and selfish ambition can be plainly read in the unhappy careers of Jakob's father and brothers. They treated him without mercy and with contempt, and yet in human worth they could not hold a candle to him. They won worldly success, but their echo has died like that of a sounding brass, for they had not charity.

Barbara, too, who comes closest to Jakob, cannot sell what she has and follow him. She is a dualistic nature, more complex than she appears at first sight, one of Grillparzer's most impressive women. A "Mädchen aus dem Volke," a younger sister of Anna Margaret, even more inarticulate than she, Barbara personifies the unplumbed deeps and potentialities of the "Volksseele" which fascinated the Romanticists—to whom, in some ways, Grillparzer still belonged. Barbara's song, too, which becomes Jakob's "Schicksalslied," is typical of the "Volk" and their naïve and indiscriminate taste; for this is no authentic folksong but a modern sentimental ditty.[15] Nevertheless, it represents the "romantic" capacities of Barbara's untutored mind, her instinctive reaching for the higher life which Jakob comes to personify for her. It becomes the bond of their souls and of their memory of each other and their brief romance. For the poet, it is a literary device used with consummate because sparing skill: once to conclude Jakob's own story and close the "inner" frame, and once more to conclude his life: for it is the last thing that his dying ears seem to hear, like echoes from a distant shore.[16]

Under her gruff exterior, Barbara possesses a femininity and tenderness that are the more touching because they are rarely displayed. She has a deep capacity for love that is never really tapped. Though in personal traits she bears but a distant resemblance to Kathi Fröhlich, she doubtless exemplifies, on a deeper psychological level, the problem Woman in Grillparzer's consciousness, a mordant self-accusation for his failure to consummate his own relation with Kathi. Barbara is probably both a "Wunschbild" and a "Schreckbild," exhibiting a strength of character and resolute adjustment to life such as he envied, and at the same time a masterfulness such as he could not brook in women.

There is a singular kinship between Barbara and Jakob, for all their difference in class and education. Both are completely honest and honorable (she, to be sure, in a more practical way than her guileless lover); both are unselfish, conscientious, order-loving—"Ordnung" is a frequent motif in the portrayals of both—and fond of music (Barbara in a wholly naïve, folk way). Both are motherless, and in nature at variance with their fathers.

Barbara attracts men physically, but in Jakob she meets the only man who respects her as an autonomous spiritual being and equal, and who opens up a higher intellectual life to her, appealing to her latent tenderness and love of beauty. Her tragedy follows from the fact that this man, to whom she would fain join her life, fails her in the masculine qualities of strength, assertiveness, and mastery of life that could assure her an existence on the higher plane of which he has given her a glimpse. So she has to make a choice which would have been routine and not painful had he never crossed her path. Her parting arraignment of him is a mixture of frustration, resentment, and self-pity, but also compassion for him; it is the epitaph of an unrealized life: "Sie haben es selbst gewollt, sich und uns haben Sie unglücklich gemacht; aber freilich sich selbst am meisten. Eigentlich verdienen Sie kein Mitleid ... Wenn man so schwach ist ... Ist's doch Ihr Werk. Ich muss nun hinaus unter die groben Leute, wogegen ich mich so lange gesträubt habe" (75). Outwardly, and according to the standards of her class, she does the sensible thing in giving up Jakob and marrying the country butcher, but from the point of view of her finer potentialities she has taken second-best. She throws in her lot with "reality" and material security, while Jakob persists in his dream. But she, the strong, is defeated in her "success," while he, the weak, remains triumphant in his "failure."

As Brentano in old Anna Margaret, so Grillparzer in old Jakob has created a character whose spiritual calm and moral integrity he himself yearns to possess; and in the present case the blood-tie between the ideal figure and the author is much closer and more tragic. Jakob has from the beginning what Medea prays for in vain: "Lass uns die Götter bitten um ein einfach Herz;" and he achieves early what Rustan declares to be the only possible happiness on earth: "des Innern stiller Frieden/ Und die schuldbefreite Brust." Jakob's sleep is that of an infant. One imagines him, even as a youth, with that serene smile of "ungetrübte Heiterkeit" which the narrator first perceives on his face in the public park and which is on his face when he dies (41, 79).

This story, then, which is a landmark of the new realism—how many generations have discovered the "real" world anew!—which depicts so clearly the realities of things and people in its time and place, vindicates after all the higher reality of ideas. What Tieck might have demonstrated in *Des Lebens Überfluss* had he believed in his own ideal and not begged the question with a clap-trap *deus ex machina* at the end; what Novalis and the "dated" Romantic idealists were convinced of, the primacy of mind over "fact," is here impressively realized with the methods of pure poetic art:

> The mind is its own place, and in itself
> Can make a heaven of hell, a hell of heaven.

CHAPTER SEVEN

KELLER, *ROMEO UND JULIA AUF DEM DORFE* (1856)

Gottfried Keller, one of the greatest masters of Poetic Realism and of the Novelle, seems never to have distinguished in theory between the Novelle and the novel. He was not a theorist, but a practitioner. His lack of formal education was in this respect a blessing, that it made him less anxious about precedents and "rules." One inevitably compares him with his great contemporary and fellow-townsman Meyer. Both of them became exemplary "Novellisten," but their art was as different as their family origins. Keller is more the naïve genius, Meyer the highly cultured talent. Using Schiller's critical categories, one could differentiate them as "naiv" and "sentimentalisch," or even better as "musikalisch" and "plastisch." Keller is the born story-teller, of fecund imagination; his rich inventiveness amounts at times to a fault. Meyer is a much more careful husbandman of his more limited resources. Keller originates characters and lavishes a wealth of invention upon them. Meyer, the conscious stylist, is far less originative, preferring to give exquisite shape to matter preformed for him by history and art. Keller once referred to Meyer's work as "brocade;" one could fancy Meyer retorting that Keller's fabric was homespun. There are occasional small flaws in Keller's weave. One cannot well imagine the meticulous Meyer letting stand a sentence like the following, with its four "welche:" "Sie horchten ein Weilchen auf diese eingebildeten oder wirklichen Töne, welche von der grossen Stille herrührten oder welche sie mit den magischen Wirkungen des Mondlichtes verwechselten, welches nah und fern über die weissen Herbstnebel wallte, welche tief auf den Gründen lagen."[1] On the other hand, one would not find in Meyer the imaginative, synaesthetic Romanticism of this passage and its musical overtones, nor the warmth and depth of passion that makes the lovers in *Romeo und Julia* so real.

There are qualities in Keller's style that make against the ideal spareness of the Novelle. His fancy has a "barock" robustiousness. He delights in bodying forth a gallery of "wunderliche Heilige" like the bankrupt Seldwylers at their fishing (115-116). He sets before us in all her idiosyncrasy a vociferous and gullible "Bäuerin" and lets her empty head be filled with a delicious and detailed fabrication (153-157). He gives us a bitterly comical picture of Mrs. Manz as a hostess (112-113). This is justifiable, to be sure, as comic relief and tragic irony in a high and special sense. Such bold mingling of comic and tragic is what Heyse had in mind when he called Keller "ein Shakespeare der Novelle." And seemingly gratuitous figures like the substantial "Wirtin" and her spiteful waitress (163-164) might be said to help characterize the heroine. More dispensable, for the strictest economy of the Novelle, are the many comments and observations with which the author accompanies his tale and anticipates its outcome. Keller did not aspire to complete objectivity, and he even acknowledged a moral purpose in literature. The lovingly elaborated interlude of the playing children (87-88, 91-95), marvellously real and unsentimentalized—an incredible achievement for a childless and lonely bachelor—could well have been spared, so far as the structural needs of the Novelle are concerned, and yet, having once followed this vivid sequence, one would be loth to miss it. And one may see in the children's play both the obvious picture of a primeval paradise and, more deeply, the manifestation of that very force of human cruelty (die menschliche Grausamkeit in den Kindern, 93f.) that will later bar their return to their chosen world.

Keller himself never referred to this work as a Novelle, but merely as an "Erzählung" or "Geschichte." Yet it embodies the basic desiderata of a Novelle. It has one crucial conflict around which the plot is organized. It has a small number of characters. It has, about midway, a definite "Wendepunkt:" Sali's striking of Marti, with unforeseen and fateful consequences. It has symbolic leitmotifs, chiefly the stone-pile on the disputed triangle of land and the Black Fiddler, either of which could qualify as a "Falke." An "Idee" could be found in the brief newspaper item which was Keller's actual starting-point and which, in slightly altered form, concludes his story—though to be sure this summarizes ironically his bald "source" rather than what he made of it. It contains, however, the element of paradox which is so often implicit in the subject-matter of Novellen. The "Rahmen" in this case is minimal, being restricted to one paragraph at the beginning and one at the end, both really dispensable.[2]

Yet Keller, like all the great masters of the Novelle beginning with Kleist, while maintaining the general type, has enlarged and deepened it in a new way. He has shown that the Novelle can be made the medium for one of the great themes of the world's literature and, treating this theme in terms of his familiar homeland and its plain folk, he has given a superlative example both of "Heimatkunst" and of middle-class tragedy. He pictures virtually the whole lifetime of his two chief personages from infancy to death—evincing as fine an understanding of the psychology of adolescence as of childhood—and in addition conveys an impression of their entire surrounding world. He condenses the essential substance of a novel into a Novelle of one hundred pages, and he does this in the main by throwing light on certain critical turns in the protracted action.

We see the children first when they are respectively seven and five, and the fathers, about forty, are in their prime of prosperity. Then several years are allowed to elapse rapidly; the children are now ten and eight, then eleven and nine. Almost ten years of litigation are summarized in a few pages (102-104). At the time of the tragic finale, Sali and Vrenchen have reached twenty and eighteen, the fathers are on in their fifties. Keller has not carried the scene-technique so far as Annette did in the *Judenbuche*: he has fewer and longer "pictures" and his procedure is more strictly narrative and less directly dramatic.

It is surprising, in view of the seemingly complete social background of the story, that important institutions such as school and church play no part in it, any more than they do in the *Judenbuche*. We see no teacher nor pastor nor playmates. Very little is made of the neighbors, and that only negatively. But one can read *Romeo und Julia* many times without noticing the absence of these things. It is the tendency of the Novelle to focus on the center of its world and to leave the rest, as some modern photographs do, in a grey and indistinct tone. The art of the Novelle-writer is one of isolating and enhancing, in such a way as to give the effect of an unbroken whole.

Romeo und Julia is an excellent example of Poetic Realism, showing how its Romantic heritage is blended with a sharpened sense for the hard realities of everyday life. Keller has a certain amount of Romantic imagination, even a Romantic love for the extraordinary and bizarre; but his imagination never runs away with him; it is restrained by an unerring sense of fact. His landscape pictures in this story, as in so many of his actual watercolors, are full of definitely outlined reality, overlaid with the dreamy blue haze of the "romantische Landschaft." His theme is the "romantic" one of Romeo and Juliet, but it is set in the harsh workaday reality of a Swiss peasant village. Yet the language throughout, though lifelike, is held to a certain level, and this is characteristic of Poetic Realism. These peasants do not speak a dialect (a few Swiss idioms do occur), and they never descend to vulgarity, even in moments of anger. The Romantic note of "Vergänglichkeit" is struck, the pathos of the transiency of all beauty is borne in upon us: "wenn das Küssen zweier Verliebter auf eine oder zwei Minuten sich selbst überlebt und die Vergänglichkeit alles Lebens mitten im Rausche der Blütezeit ahnen lässt" (135). The Romantic "Liebestod" motif that runs from Novalis to Wagner here receives one of its most beautiful embodiments, in the plain garb of humble life.

It is the way of the Poetic Realist to observe accurately the things of actuality, but to select certain of their traits for an artistic purpose and raise these into a higher, significant reality. There is a wonderfully sharp quality, a *plein-air* lighting, in the opening scene of the two peasants plowing over a rise of ground in the bright sun of a September morning (85-87). As we draw near, the figures show the distinct and characteristic detail of a portrait. We see the lines in the men's well-shaven faces, the creases in their breeches, the jarring of their shirt-sleeves as they hold the plow. Keller points up their type-likeness by calling our attention to the one differentiating feature of their cap-tassels, blown opposite ways by the wind, and to the precise "middle instant" when the tassels flash heavenward simultaneously like two white flames. Then he likens them to two constellations rising and setting behind earth's round, thus accenting their exemplary character and suggesting a deeper significance behind their doings.

The manifest symmetrical patterning of the whole story is an element of the "poetic" superimposed on the "real." At the end of the day's plowing, the two men at the same instant take their first overt step on the road of wrong-doing: each cuts a sizable furrow beyond his line into the intervening field; and as they do so the motif of the white tassels and the constellations is repeated and then varied with the kindred motif of the weavers' shuttles: "Was er webt, das weiss kein Weber:" (95-96). Much later, the astral motif is picked up again with antiphonal effect in the harmonious constellation of the children, soon to be "crossed" by the baleful "dark star" of the Black Fiddler (129). All this is reality, not falsified, but seen and selected with a poet's and philosopher's eye that invests mere fact with higher meaning.

In the account of the Manzes' removal to town and in the picture of the wretched "inn" which they take over (109-111), the realistic details are carefully chosen to contribute to the oppressive atmosphere of deterioration. The same is true of the corresponding picture of Marti's run-down farm (124-126), where the neglected well is singled out as a special "symbol of shiftlessness." But Keller shows a painter's appreciation for the picturesque aspects of this dilapidation, and he even humanizes them. It is the painter likewise who puts the red wreath of poppies into the dark, curly hair of the brunette Vrenchen (Keller himself refers to this as a painting, 135), or sets the black figure of the Fiddler on top of the stone-pile covered with the same fiery-red flowers (130)—a striking symbol of the unhappy past invading the happy present of new-found love. In the detailed description of the "Paradiesgärtlein," a former country villa now become a cheap dance resort, Keller emphasizes features that highlight the picture of grotesque decay (170f.). The types of the dancers there are clearly brought out by a few graphic traits (173f.).

Since Poetic Realism aims to show not merely objects but significant objects, things that have a meaning beyond their mere factual presence, it passes readily into Symbolism. There is a good deal of symbolism in *Romeo und Julia*. For example, the stones which the two men plow up out of the stolen land, they throw onto the ever-narrowing middle field on which Sali and Vrenchen played as children. Soon the ridge of stones and the wild growth on it are so high that the two young people, though grown, can no longer see each other across it. Thus the fathers' misdeed has raised a barrier between their families (96). Manz, when he acquires the field, has all these stones dumped on the disputed triangle at one corner of it, thus raising a monument, "ein schönes Denkmal," as Keller ironically terms it, to their common wrong-doing (101). In Marti's neglected garden an ancient halberd, a family heirloom, has to serve, along with rake-handles and broomsticks, to hold up the beans (126). The venerable weapon, betokening the honorable past of the family, shares its degradation. Vrenchen, when she leaves forever the house where she was born, hangs its rusty key on a scroll of the halberd (157), thus appointing it the last guardian of those age-old family traditions which persist so tragically as ideals in the minds of the children.

Keller's chief problem, and his chief triumph, in *Romeo und Julia* was that of motivation. There have been, early and late, critics unwilling to accept the tragic outcome as inevitable, and even ready to condemn it as immoral. In the original version, Keller himself, in one of those concluding "caudal appendages" which Heyse wisely amputated, defended himself against the charge of palliating or glorifying the lovers' suicide, and conceded that a life of quiet renunciation and labor, combined with the effects of time, might have made things come out right after all (396)! Here, one feels, the Swiss moralist and pedagogue Keller, loth to admit limits to the powers of education, does injustice to the poet's masterly creation. For the plot of *Romeo und Julia*, within its established premises of character and situation, is flawless, and this simple tale moves to its end with all the inevitableness of high tragedy. The stern lines of its inherent necessity are beautified, but never effaced, by the poetic delicacy of Keller's treatment and the sustained purity of the lovers' passion.

The motivation rests, for one thing, on the characters. There are the fathers, Manz and Marti, dour, taciturn, tenacious peasants, with their avaricious love of the "good earth" (89) and their inflexible stubbornness, even in a cause they know to be bad. They are not villains, they do no greater wrong at the start than most of their neighbors would have done under like circumstances. But once having compromised with evil, they go on consistently, weaving the unpredictable pattern of their destiny on the loom of fate (96). There are the mothers, one of whom, being of finer stuff, soon succumbs to grief over the deterioration of her family, the other of whom adapts herself and becomes a part of the deleterious home atmosphere that surrounds these "star-cross'd lovers." There is Manz's son, Sali, young, uncounselled, again and again "ratlos" and "verwirrt" before the new experiences which fate crowds into a single day (162), yet endowed with the dogged single-mindedness of his peasant forebears; capable of deep passion, incapable of long repression and renunciation (175f.), and ready, with the uncompromising idealism of youth, for extreme measures.

The most important character is Vrenchen, and her temperament is an indispensable factor in the tragic motivation. Already as a child, she is "ein feuriges Dirnchen" (96). At sixteen, with her flashing dark eyes, her cheeks and lips suffused with crimson, her dusky, exotic complexion, she suggests an Italian Juliet: "feurige Lebenslust und Fröhlichkeit zitterte in jeder Fiber dieses Wesens" (106). She is a naturally gay, high-spirited, sensuous creature, "ein lustiges, feuriges Wesen," with a resilient joyousness that rebounds at the slightest relief from her load of cares (106, 132, 140). She is capable of amorous mischievousness; she falls readily into the role of an ardent bride; there is even a hint of possible future unfaithfulness on her part (165, 178). Of the two lovers, she is the more passionate. For her, the consummation of their love becomes an all-absorbing desire, a matter of life and death, and she fires Sali with her own passionate volition (183). That she, who at important turns in the action leads and initiates, is of such a sensuous, ardent nature, is one of the conditions of Keller's tragedy.

As she is the first to awaken to love, she is also the first to sense its hopeless termination (136, 139). The note of death is struck long before the end, and the author leaves us in no doubt as to the goal of his action, which indeed is presaged by his very title. He links life and death in a mystical-Romantic fashion, and the love of these children, flowering in the shadow of their families' ruin, gains a strange beauty and lustre from its sombre foil. Premonitions and symbols are employed to prepare us for coming events: Sali's mother is uneasy at his going; Sali feels moved to take special leave of his parents and home (149, 150); Vrenchen gathers the last flowers from her garden, and when death is near, they wither and die at her breast; she casts them on the stream that is soon to receive her body and her lover's (184f.). In dancing, she crushes the gingerbread house that childishly symbolized marital hopes which are never to be fulfilled (171f.).

There is a more suggestive symbolism in the poor rings they buy for each other, ostensibly as parting-gifts, yet with a subconscious intuition of their eventual function as wedding-tokens. Vrenchen's persistent idea of dancing is prepared for by her dream, which in turn is the manifest betrayal of the wish to marry: "wir tanzten zusammen auf unserer Hochzeit, lange, lange Stunden" (145f.). The specifically suggestive words of the Black Fiddler as he advocates the vagabond life arouse Sali's emotions (178f.). Vrenchen is equally stirred by the hostess's assumption that she is a bride and by her own deliberate acting of this part: "das Brautwesen lohte ihm im Blute, und je hoffnungsloser es war, umso wilder und unbezwinglicher" (179). There is a potent suggestion in the open amorousness of the couples about them at the dance. The mock marriage-ceremony performed by the Fiddler, though they profess not to take it seriously, nevertheless affects them deeply. The excitation of the wild bacchantic procession tells on them both, especially Vrenchen, and is the final suggestive element in a sinister situation.

But *Romeo und Julia* is not merely the tragedy of young and ill-starred love; it is also a "middle-class tragedy," a "bürgerliches Trauerspiel" of impressive proportions and compelling motivation. It deals with social deterioration and loss of caste and the unhappy consequences thereof in two generations.

Keller begins, therefore, with a picture of the state from which these people are to fall. Everything on his opening pages contributes to the impression of prosperous, self-sufficient, seemingly impregnable respectability. He exhibits two peasants plowing with fine teams on large, splendid fields—two of the leading peasants of their community (97), steady, self-confident, well-cared-for men in the prime of life, who stand and work on their native soil with calm assurance, perfect specimens of the ancient indigenous type that sets the standard for the land (86). Perhaps the most characterizing adjective the author applies to them is "sicher," a word that recurs like a refrain (86, 119, 159, 176), indicating an important element in their ideal of life.

Self-satisfied and "standessicher," they look with contempt upon the neighboring townsmen, "die Lumpenhunde zu Seldwyl" (88). The Black Fiddler, whose ownership of the intervening field they deny, is beyond the pale of their sympathy since his parents descended to the class of vagrants. From such a descent there is, in their opinion, no return; they are merciless in their disdain for the unpropertied classes. It is significant that, as soon as their enmity has developed, each one sees in it an imputation of social inferiority: his opponent must necessarily think him a poor, defenseless wretch—such as the Fiddler—to dare put such wrongs upon him, "da man dergleichen etwa einem armen haltlosen Teufel, nicht aber einem aufrechten, klugen und wehrhaften Manne gegenüber sich erlauben könne" (102).

"Reality" for these two men is their passionate delusion, as Keller tells us in a Dantean figure: "ihr Leben glich fortan der träumerischen Qual zweier Verdammten, welche, auf einem schmalen Brette einen dunklen Strom hinabtreibend, sich befehden, in die Luft hauen und sich selber anpacken und vernichten, in der Meinung, sie hätten ihr Unglück gefasst" (102).

Having embarked on a wrong course, they pursue it obstinately. They get into the clutches of shyster lawyers and speculators; they alter their mode of life radically, yet with a troubled conscience; they deteriorate by rapid stages (Verarmung, Verschlechterung, Verfall, 104). But the first overt step of declassment, which the author in his own person condemns, is taken by Manz when he abandons his farm to become a tavern-keeper in the hitherto despised town (109). Before long he is reduced to fishing, the occupation of Seldwyla's failures.

Marti, meanwhile, has remained ostensibly a farmer, but is completely ostracized: no one has anything to do with him and his daughter, and no one lends them a hand in their need. With the careful symmetry which is a striking structural feature of this story, Keller gives us a realistic picture of Marti's ruined farm that balances an equally unsparing picture of Manz's dubious "Spelunke." Finally Marti too must take up fishing, "die verkehrte Wasserpfuscherei" (125).

In this pursuit, the former friends meet and fight, in a scene that forms the climax of this domestic drama, a scene that for all its rustic limitations comes near to the grandiose. The gathering and breaking thunderstorm, which forms such an imposing background and parallel to the nicely balanced human action, is not mere stage-setting, but is integrated, like everything else, into the motivation: the men are out in this weather because it is favorable for fishing (117), and their encounter comes about naturally. Equally natural and deeply moving is the unfolding of the children's love at the moment of their fathers' direst hatred.

Marti becomes at least a potential criminal, while Manz becomes a harborer of criminals and receiver of stolen goods. Both have now arrived at "gänzliche Verkommenheit" (141), but Marti is more drastically erased from bourgeois society by becoming a public charge in an asylum for the insane. His trip there, and his imbecilic antics, are realistically reported (140-142). He is now an "armer Tropf," at the other end of the social scale from the class-conscious, prosperous peasant of the beginning.

The enmity of the fathers, and the decline resulting from it, blights the lives of the children. Sali and Vrenchen would have suffered severely from the mere decay of their families, even if they had never fallen in love with each other. The tragedy of social deterioration precedes and underlies the love-tragedy. Keller tells us expressly that their youth is spoiled and their future made hopeless by the very "Verfall" induced by their fathers' quarrel (105, 108).

It is their unhappy lot to remember clearly the former prosperity of their houses, and this memory bulks large in the *impasse* they finally reach. Like exiles from a childhood paradise, they take with them an ideal of what life should be, and when they cannot attain or recover this ideal state, they despair. Sali retains a definite picture of his father as he once was, a substantial, shrewd, and staid peasant (107). Keller subtly indicates the tragedy inherent in the ideal of class and family continuities by making Sali a pretty exact replica of his father; the latter, in his turn, is tormented by the memory of what he once was, and involuntarily respects in his son his own irretrievable youth (107f.).

Even before Sali has done disastrous injury to Vrenchen's father, it is clear that the parents' strife and its economic and social consequences will prevent a happy union of the children. To Sali's suggestion of close friendship, Vrenchen at once answers hopelessly: "Und unsere Eltern?" And when Sali protests, like Schiller's Max, that they are not answerable for what their parents have done and become, and voices, like Shakespeare's Friar, the hope that their love alone may repair their families' fortunes, she replies with gloomy conviction that no good can ever come of it: "Es wird nie gut kommen, geh in Gottes Namen deiner Wege!" (127). Later, when marriage is hinted at, they both immediately become dejected at the thought of their future blighted by the enmity of their parents (136f.). All this precedes Sali's striking of Marti.

In the symbolical figure of the Black Fiddler, this inescapable shadow of parental guilt soon falls on the children's budding hopes. The Fiddler and the ominous "Steinhaufen" on the debated triangle of land recur as leitmotifs and symbols of inherited sin. Again and again we are reminded of that initial wrong as the germ of the whole tragic development. The black fellow last appears dancing and fiddling wildly in the nocturnal orgies on the "Steinhaufen," a Hoffmannesque *genius loci*, personifying the fathers' guilt at the very spot of their original transgression and knitting the end of the tragic web cogently and spectacularly to its beginning (180).

Romeo und Julia is pure bourgeois tragedy, in the sense of Hebbel's *Maria Magdalene*: the tragic conflict is no longer, as it was in Schiller's *Kabale und Liebe*, a conflict between the middle and a higher social class, but a conflict within the middle class itself; it is based on the tragic limitedness of the bourgeois mind, immolating itself to its own ideals of respectability. Keller, however, has made these ideals more admirable, and treated the theme more poetically, than has Hebbel.

To these young people, with the ingrained convictions of their class, the mere dissension and degradation of their elders present a formidable barrier. To this is added Sali's act of violence against Marti, which creates an insuperable ethical obstacle to their union. Vrenchen recognizes this instantly: "Es ist aus, es ist ewig aus, wir können nicht zusammenkommen!" (139). Their economic and social scruples are now supplemented by a moral scruple; and no decent marriage, according to their standards, can be built on this foundation. Vrenchen is conscious of both the old and the new difficulties when she says: "I can never have you, even if there were not all the other reasons, simply because you struck my father and deprived him of his reason. That would always be a bad foundation-stone for our marriage, and we two should never be free from care, never!" (144).

They therefore resolve to separate, though they feel they cannot long survive the separation. First, however, they plan to have one last day together; and this day brings experiences which wholly upset their conscious calculations. They taste for a few brief hours the privileges of a state of society from which they see themselves forever excluded, and this, together with suggestions from their immediate environment, brings them to the desperate decision to drain the cup of their love and end their lives. Since they cannot be united in an irreproachable bourgeois marriage, and cannot live without each other, there remains for them only death together.

It is a day of tragic make-believe. They shut their eyes to the coming separation and give themselves over to the deep joy of being together, "neatly dressed and free, like two happy people who rightfully belong to each other" (158). They resume instinctively the manners of the class to which they rightfully belong; they are modest, considerate, dignified, "sittig," "ehrbar," "fein und ordentlich" (160, 162). They play convincingly the part of "respectable young people" (159), "as though they did not come from houses filled with quarreling and misery, but were children of substantial folk, walking along with the fairest hopes" (160). Vrenchen is the neat, decorous young "Bäuerin;" Sali is not the son of a degenerate alehouse-keeper, but the well-to-do young farmer inspecting his woods (160, 162). They feel a kindred satisfaction in watching the well-ordered, "sicher" activity in a prosperous inn (158f.). Vrenchen would fain linger here, to prolong the dream, "um wenigstens auf Stunden sich an einem stattlichen Orte zu Hause zu träumen" (159). At the second inn, they again manifest their natural attraction to solid "ordentliche Leute" and their ways (163).

They make one last attempt at reinstatement. But intolerant society, represented by persons of their own age and former class, opposes to them a rigid wall which is no less impenetrable for being a conglomerate of embarrassment, pity, contempt, and envy (169). They are rebuffed; instead of dancing at the substantial inn where they belong by right of class and instinct, they must descend to the "Paradiesgärtlein:" "Wir wollen gehen, wo das arme Volk sich lustig macht, zu dem wir jetzt auch gehören, da werden sie uns nicht verachten" (170). They have now been demoted to the society of the poor and lowly, "die Kinder der ganz kleinen Bauern und Tagelöhner und sogar mancherlei fahrendes Gesinde," "verlumpte Leute aus Seldwyla, . . . armes Volk von allen Enden" (170, 172). When these have left, they are alone with the outright rabble, "das eigentliche Hudelvölkchen," the scum of society as they knew it, the class to which their fathers once denied all civil rights save burial (173, 90). And—crowning irony—they are glad to be patronized by the Fiddler whom their fathers had once chased off their farms (131).

He proposes to the distracted lovers a way out: the free, irresponsible, licentious life of his gypsy band. But to both Sali and Vrenchen this mode of life is repugnant; they could never reconcile it with their bourgeois ideas (177f.). However much they yearn for union, they will not have it on these terms.

Near the end of his story (175f.), Keller summarizes the irresistible forces that are closing in on the young lovers, and the one he makes the most of is their frustrated craving for an irreproachable bourgeois station in life. "The feeling that in the bourgeois world one could be happy only in a completely honorable marriage with a clear conscience, was just as lively in [Sali] as in Vrenchen; and in both these forsaken souls it was the last flicker of the honor which had burned brightly in their houses in earlier times and which the self-confident fathers had extinguished and destroyed through an insignificant mistake when they, under the delusion that they could augment this very honor by increase of their property, so thoughtlessly and, as they thought, so safely took to themselves the property of a missing man."

Thus the tragic circle is completed: the final result of the fathers' seemingly slight misstep at the end of that day's plowing years ago, is now at hand. The very vestige of "bürgerliches Ehrgefühl" which persists in the children after the decay of their families, is what brings about their destruction. Had they been less honorable, less bound by the code of honor proper to their class, there would have been for them no tragedy nor death. But they have cherished in their minds the original "Urmass" of what constitutes the desirable life. Indeed, one reason for their passionate and utter love is that each sees in the other the incorporation of fortune and happiness lost but never forgotten: "Als sie sich wiederfanden, sahen sie in sich zugleich das verschwundene Glück des Hauses, und beider Neigung klammerte sich nur umso heftiger ineinander" (176f.).

They thirst for happiness, but only on reputable bourgeois conditions: "Sie mochten so gern fröhlich und glücklich sein, aber nur auf einem guten Grund und Boden, und dieser schien ihnen unerreichbar" (177). But neither will their fiery passion be denied, and so they take the way out which to them, and to the reader who has followed Keller's presentation of the situation, must seem the only way out. The marvel is that to this very end, in the midst of their glowing passion and their wicked environment, the poet has kept his pair innocent and pure. He has thus made their fate deeply pathetic, yet genuinely tragic; they exemplify that maturest species of tragedy in which a character is ruined not by outward circumstances merely, but by his own mind and will, and not by his worse, but by his better nature.

By contrast, the lovers in Schiller's *Wallenstein,* Max and Thekla, are not organically connected with the world of their parents; indeed, they are hardly credible as children of these parents. They represent an ideal order of morality, superimposed on sordid reality; they have been grown in the nursery of Schiller's idealism and transplanted into this rude and alien soil, there to bloom briefly and perish, illustrating "das Los des Schönen auf der Erde." Keller's lovers, on the other hand, are not the product of philosophical abstraction, but are firmly rooted in their native earth. They have fully accepted their parents' pristine standards; they are bone of their bone and flesh of their flesh. This makes them truly tragic, whereas Schiller's pair remain pathetic victims, a prey to the selfishness and wrong-doing of others.

Without entering upon detailed comparisons and contrasts, one can point out that Keller's *Romeo und Julia,* in its character as a "bürgerliches Trauerspiel," differs decidedly from Shakespeare's *Romeo and Juliet,* which is exclusively a tragedy of love. Shakespeare needed to go no further back than the beginning of the love-relationship. The "ancient grudge" of the two families is an initial assumption; Montague and Capulet are listed among the *Persons* as "heads of two houses at variance with each other." The enmity of these two men and their followers is at battle pitch when the action opens. For Keller, on the other hand, it was important to show by what stages the hostility developed, long before the children's love emerged; by what steps these two families declined from their original estate. Shakespeare begins, and ends, with "two households, both alike in dignity;" the element of declassment is not a part of his problem at all. The interest is focused on Romeo and Juliet and their love; the parents are colorless and ineffectual. Keller delineates the parents clearly; their personalities and their deterioration are an essential part of his problem. Shakespeare can compress his action into a few days; Keller must stretch his over a dozen years or more.

Romeo's killing of Tybalt is comparable as a tragic motive to Sali's injuring of Vrenchen's father. In both cases, violence is done by the young hero, under virtually irresistible provocation, to a near kinsman of the heroine, and an irremovable shadow is thereby thrown over the lovers' association. But Keller has intensified tragically both the nearness of the blood-relationship and the ethical import of the hero's act. The obstacle, with Keller, exists only within the lovers' consciousness: Sali's act, unlike Romeo's, is not publicly known, and not the slightest suspicion falls on him. Romeo is exiled by the prince's decree; Sali and Vrenchen are shut out from life by the ideals and prejudices and scruples of their own middle-class minds. In this story, then, with its realistic depiction of social environment, we have another vindication of the superior reality of the "world within."

On the pre-established basis of family enmity, Shakespeare builds his tragedy, with the help of much chance and contrivance. Keller's Novelle is simpler in structure, and its motivation must seem, to the modern reader at least, more plausible. His events follow one another naturally, without hurry, without a hint of artifice. His love-plot does not depend on an incredible potion or a convenient pestilence; and moreover it is supported by a cogent social plot, the plot of a genuine "middle-class tragedy."

It is conceivable that Shakespeare's lovers might have "lived happily ever after," had they escaped from the particular combination of circumstances that here beset them; the method is indicated by Friar Laurence in the third scene of the third act; the slaying of Tybalt raises no such barrier as does Sali's corresponding deed; the somewhat perfunctory hatred of Montagues and Capulets seems, at the end, to have evaporated. But Keller's peasant lovers could never have escaped their tragedy, because they could never have escaped from themselves.

CHAPTER EIGHT

MEYER, *DER HEILIGE* (1879)

Conrad Ferdinand Meyer was one of the finest of German stylists in prose and verse. He wrought with utmost care and consciousness. His imagination tended toward a pictorial and dramatic, even sculptural visualization of scenes and figures. His artistic ideal was sharply delineated objectivity; his means were restriction, concentration, symbolization, and scrupulous economy of expression. He strove for the pregnant and lapidary, but he achieved it in most cases only after painstaking recasting and filing. He had a predilection for the commanding figures and great, decisive events of history. All these traits and ideals would seem to qualify him pre-eminently to be a master of the Novelle, and in particular the historical Novelle. And in fact he has no peer in German narrative literature in the artistic reanimation of history.

Meyer seems to have been an "eidetic," that is, he saw things habitually in pictures. History transformed itself for him into a series of "Bilder und Gestalten," which he beheld with the eye almost of a painter or sculptor. Schiller, too, saw history in terms of the leaders, and his accounts of it tended to become a sequence of great biographies; but he saw it with the eye of the philosopher, the moralist, and the pseudo-professional historian. Meyer sees it from a more purely artistic point of view and a more modern psychological one. His attitude is as sovereign as Schiller's. "Die Geschichte benutze ich natürlich nach Möglichkeit," he said to Adolf Frey in regard to *Der Heilige*, "verfahre aber ganz souverän mit ihr, indem ich nicht ruhe, bevor ich das Materielle der Historie der Willkür der Poesie unterworfen habe."[1]

In Thierry's *Histoire de la conquête de l'Angleterre par les Normands*, which he read in Lausanne as early as 1853, he had come upon the "rätselhafte Figur" of Thomas Becket—so he tells us in an autobiographical sketch—"und ich habe so lange an ihr herumgebildet, bis sie mir fast quälend vor den Augen stand," and the writing of his Novelle became an act of liberation from this phantom.[2] To the writer Betty Paoli, Meyer spoke of his hero as his own creation, born of his very soul and having no real analogue in history.[3] Though he had read Thierry's account and a few related sources years before, he apparently took care *not* to make any *ad hoc* "Vorstudien" preliminary to writing,[4] but to let the mysterious process of subconscious cerebration hold undisturbed sway. Later, when his interpretation of Becket was questioned, he could reply simply: "Die Wahrheit ist, dass ich den Thomas *so sah*. Damit gut."[5]

Der Heilige shows the German Novelle in a new capacity: that of giving, or vividly suggesting, the picture of a whole age of history, with its great personages and its great problems: here, the relations of Church and State, the relations of different races, conquerors and conquered, in the same country; the ethics of government; the question of loyalty and treason. Meyer may well claim to have introduced "den grossen Stil"—if not of tragedy, as he thought, certainly of major history—into the Novelle. In consequence, his story is strikingly long, a full two hundred pages in the standard edition, more than ten times the length of *Der tolle Invalide*.

But *Der Heilige* is indubitably a Novelle and not a novel. It is so organized that all its parts "look toward the center."[6] Persons and events are not given in the full round of the novel, but are only illuminated on the side which they show to the participants in the action; there is a notable compression and economy of narration. Exactly in the middle of the story comes the "Wendepunkt" in the shape of Henry's resolve to raise Thomas to the Primacy, despite the latter's warning, and therewith the beginning of radical changes in Thomas. A "Falke" is present in the person of Becket's daughter Gnade, whose name and fate at the same time furnish a principal "Leitmotiv." Her death is the critical "Ereignis" of the narrative; it occurs comparatively early, but because of Becket's secretive character and peculiar relation to his King, is slow in showing its effects. The substance of the story is summarizable in brief and characteristically paradoxical formulation.[7] The plot involves a small number of mature individuals, whose latent potentialities are revealed under the stress of an extraordinary happening. In this case, since the Novelle is a historical one, there are an unusual number of incidental characters; but these are kept in the limbo of the setting, outside the field of central focus. The "frame," less ornate than that in *Die Hochzeit des Mönchs* (where it is something of a *tour de force*), is Meyer's most artistic and successful one.

Meyer's favorite ground was the period of Reformation and

Renaissance. Most of his stories are laid in the 16th and 17th centuries and in Romance lands. *Der Heilige,* then, in going back to 12th-century England, represents a new departure. The medieval color is skilfully produced, above all in the "frame" and its characters, particularly the narrator, whom Meyer is justified in calling "ein lebendiges Stück Mittelalter" (*Bfe.* II, 347). Through his lips, the author protests at being held to exact dates (148); and indeed Meyer reckoned that the device of having an action reported, after a lapse of more than twenty years, by an old and simple man, would exculpate him for various departures from historical fact (*Bfe.* II, 347).

His chief "additions" to history were the further development of the romantic legend of Becket's Saracen mother (which is found in Thierry), the invention of the *Märchen* of Prinz Mondschein (Becket at the court of Cordova), and the invention of Becket's daughter Gnade (Grace) and the entire plot connected with her—for which he presumably got a hint from the story of Fair Rosamond.

In a series of notes on his Novelle contained in a letter to the poet Lingg (*Bfe.* II, 305f.), Meyer sums up the raw material offered by history as follows: "A Norman king heaps favors upon a Saxon favorite and for political reasons makes him his Primate. The latter suddenly turns against him, and there ensues a terrible struggle between King and Bishop. The King, in other words, has been thoroughly and fearfully deceived in his favorite." Here, clearly, was an unexpected lacuna in history, an enigma which Meyer felt challenged to solve. It was a task that appealed to the connoisseur of history, the psychologist, and the delineator of poetic character. It was, in a way, like the restoration of a defaced medieval manuscript of which the end was clear, the beginning vague and legendary, the middle missing. What happened in the middle, and why, to alter so fatefully the relations of King and Chancellor-Priest?

Here was an opportunity to show the difference between the conventional estimation of a saint and the cruel reality of his actual life (*Bfe.* II, 66). There is an irony implicit in Meyer's very title, for this Saint is revealed—in a manner vastly different from Keller's in his *Sieben Legenden*—to have been anything but a saint. Here a supreme master in the poetic recreation of the past seems to call into question the very possibility of history as a true record of "reality" in the higher sense. When all is said and done, Thomas Becket remains an enigma, only a more refined one, and we are still inclined to agree with Faust: "Die Zeiten der Vergangenheit/Sind uns ein Buch mit sieben Siegeln."

There was doubtless a personal attraction for Meyer in the theme of Becket, a feeling of spiritual kinship with the man as history suggested him and even more as Meyer's own poetic power could body him forth. As already Friedrich Schlegel had pointed out, the very objectivity of the Novelle form made it an apt medium for subtle self-communication, a visible-invisible translucence of the author's "eigenste Eigentümlichkeit;"[8] and Meyer's fondness for revealing and concealing himself behind historical figures could most safely be indulged at such distance. Near the end of his productive lifetime, Meyer confessed this penchant in a letter to a French friend: "Je me sers de la forme de la nouvelle historique purement et simplement pour y loger mes expériences et mes sentiments personnels, la préférant au *Zeitroman,* parce qu'elle me masque mieux et qu'elle distance davantage le lecteur. Ainsi, sous une forme très objective et eminemment artistique, je suis au dedans tout individuel et subjectif" (*Bfe.* I, 138).

This instinctive need for "masking and distancing" was a powerful impulse toward the development of the technique of the "frame," in which Meyer became the greatest virtuoso among German "Novellisten." He wrote to Heyse: "Die Neigung zum Rahmen ... ist bei mir ganz instinktiv. Ich halte mir den Gegenstand gerne vom Leibe oder richtiger gerne so weit als möglich vom Auge" (*Bfe.* II, 340). In the case of *Der Heilige,* to be sure, Meyer subsequently assigned some quite impersonal reasons for the frame: an idyllic quality that softened the effect of a hard and cruel tale; vivifying of the historical costume; and the validation of an extraordinary character (Becket) by the eye-witness account of a man who personifies "gesunden Menschenverstand" (*Bfe.* II, 347, 306).

Certainly the author has enriched his story by the addition of the Crossbowman, and vivified the events of a distant past by reflecting them through a colorful personality interesting in its own right. Moreover, this procedure permits a focusing on the "high points" as they would stand out in the narrator's memory in the perspective of years, a "sifting" such as Poetic Realism implies.[9] And the simplicity of the man, Meyer may have felt, would make it more plausible that much of the motivation of an essentially inexplicable hero should remain unexplained. A narrator, of course, cannot be expected to know as much as an "omniscient" author; otherwise readers might ask: why not have just the latter to begin with? But Hans's position at the English court is such (and this is well motivated by his character, provenience, and previous experience) that he is present at virtually every important meeting and conversation.[10] Nowhere else has Meyer interwoven his narrator so closely with his narrative. What Hans has to tell constitutes in the main his own life-story (17); he observes correctly "mein armer Lebenslauf lässt sich von dem des Heiligen und des Königs nicht trennen" (19).

The frame of *Der Heilige* is unusual in having both a Narrator, Hans der Armbruster, and an Auditor, the old Chorherr Burkhard; contrasting types, both of them clearly individuated and set off against each other in a little proscenium action. Before the curtain rises, interest in the new Saint is aroused in several ways: in the account of a local miracle credited to him and the effect of this account on Hans; the various arguments used by his host to induce Hans to talk; Hans's dark allusions yet reluctance to tell of mysterious and unhappy things he knows— all this increases our suspense and eagerness. The initial frame is broad and elaborate: it contains the meeting and brief characterization of the two frame personages and the exposition of the local situation that furnishes the occasion for hearing about the new Saint; after fourteen pages, Hans begins his story, but this in turn has a preliminary "frame" recounting his own youth and wanderings, in the course of which he came upon the trail of Becket in Granada. Only after some twenty-five pages does the account reach England, and not for several pages after that are we launched on Becket's story proper. The Canon interrupts Hans's narration nine times; at other times, in addition, Hans addresses him with a "Herr" or "ehrwürdiger Herr," so that we are kept constantly aware of the listener and the telling of a tale. Once Hans interrupts himself to invert the sand-glass and note the coincidence of the day and hour with those of his story (188) —a little vivifying touch, a bit of medieval color, and an effective stopping for breath before the harrowing final scene.

The Auditor, the shrewd old Canon, stands in some ways for the author and for the sophisticated reader. His wish and expectation, like such a reader's, had been to be regaled, on a winter afternoon, by "ein paar Geschichtchen und Menschlichkeiten" confided by the intimate of a great man, a saint newly created, with none of the nimbus of history about him, a mere contemporary! Instead, he is confronted with a full-length, stark tragedy, the anguish of two great human lives. His reaction helps to underline for us the impressiveness of the story (195f., 206f.). The concluding frame, not so long and naturally not so suspenseful as the introductory one, returns us to the setting of the cozy room and the falling snow as the winter day, like its tale, draws to a close. What follows thereafter (192-207) is an epilogue that gathers up loose threads and brings a reposeful "Ausklingen" or diminuendo after the tempestuous and at times tormenting course of the central story.[11]

Meyer had reason to call attention to the "Reichtum der Nebenfiguren" in his story (*Bfe.* II, 306). In this rich gallery of incidental figures his fine art of characterization is seen at its best. These are deftly drawn vignettes, profiles rather than full-face portraits, a particular trait often being made to suggest the whole man. This technique is of course eminently appropriate to the restricted measure of the Novelle, and is the counterpart to the "flash-technique" of scenes we saw so masterfully employed in *Die Judenbuche.*

Meyer is especially adept in the art of introduction, the first "Auftreten" of a figure, which is often half the battle. Thus we see the narrator first as he emerges from the covered bridge (5), a rugged, monumental figure, and we get an impression of the man that never needs to be changed, though it is enriched by many details later.[12] The next moment, through his eyes, we see the auditor, Canon Burkhard, a "feine, ehrwürdige, in Marderpelz gehüllte Gestalt," as he carefully picks his way down the slushy street, looking with dismay at his wetted shoes (8). We read in his face his quick-witted plan for sounding out Hans on the subject of Becket. All the little traits we note in him by his fireside thereafter accord with this picture. He is of the type of Rat Chatillon in *Das Amulett,* and of Meyer himself: the cultured, fastidious intellectual, withdrawn from life and regarding it with a superior irony. And yet, like Hans, he is carefully kept in medieval "character."

After a suspenseful preparation we see Becket first through Hans's eyes, and the portrait, though as yet external, is entirely characteristic: the elegance, the frailty, the pallor, the grace, the seriousness, and the suggestion of Oriental origin—all are there (37). Equally determinative is King Henry's debut: his mighty physique, his imperious gesture, his piercing blue eyes, his unhesitant decision, his bright laugh (41). And thus "mein Herr und König" remains for Hans, "wie er sich mir am ersten Tage gezeigt hatte"—even to his hearty laugh (44). Of minor figures, the tall, grizzled old Armorer Rollo, "ältester Zeuge und Verkörperung des normännischen Ruhms" (199), comes in several times, and always consistent with his first appearance—a fine character-creation of Meyer's.

A different type of Norman is Gui Malherbe, another colorful invention that helps to round out the picture of the "Herrenvolk." We get an adequate conception of Queen Eleanore from a few external traits: her black "helmet" of luxuriant hair, her unsteady, "busy" eyes and "ever-hunted" feet (54). Becket's reaction to her at various junctures helps to characterize him. Richard the Lion-Hearted is brought alive in a few lapidary paragraphs (56, 150). Trustan Grimm is a subordinate figure, but, once introduced, is integrated into the action and convincingly maintained. Of the other Saxons, Äscher is briefly signalized and given an ominous note which he holds to his end (62, 85).[13] William Tracy is individualized through his "Mokierbuch" (126), and the other three slayers of Becket are likewise identified in face and gesture.

A symbolical figure, a distinguished contemporary of the kind Meyer likes to bring into his stories, is Bertram de Born, the spirit of hatred and strife, destroyer of peace, sower of dissension, and yet a poet in imagination and speech, and an unsparing exposer of the bitter truth beneath the smiling pretense of things: "So bauet denn eure Nester, rastet und scherzet im Reiche der Täuschung! . . . Mich aber lasset auffahren über den Schein in die Wahrheit der Dinge" (153). Hans's heavy "schwäbischer Seufzer" at the mockeries of Bertram and his companions, and their answering "scharfes wälsches Gelächter" (156) represent two civilizations, the Germanic and the Romanic, as Meyer saw them on their moral, not cultural, side.

Laughter is used at other times as a means of characterization. Prince John's vulgar laugh is typical of him (57, 96). King Henry laughs ingenuously (41) and heartily to the point of tears (44); he guffaws at his Chancellor's finesse (113); he snorts contemptuously to see his Queen at the Saint's feet (138); the loss of his laughter later attests the tragic deterioration of his nature. Becket is never shown laughing, and he rarely smiles (47). His daughter shares his "ernstes Lächeln" (71). His quiet, enigmatical smile is preserved even on his sepulchral monument (193f.).

Becket is by far the deepest and most complex of the characters in the story, and perhaps of all Meyer's heroes. Meyer found him an enigma in his sources, and though he made a prodigiously real person of him, he left him after all an enigma. It is to be doubted that Meyer himself entirely understood his hero. The much-admired analysis contained in his letter of May 2, 1880, to Lingg (*Bfe.* II, 305 f.) is, like most poets' *post facto* judgments of their own works, not to be taken as revealed truth and surely over-simplifies the motivation. Such "explanations" tend to be, as Meyer admitted in another letter, "dummes, nachträglich ersonnenes Zeug" (*Bfe.* II, 349), for in these cases the poet's conscious mind is trying to justify what his unconscious mind has builded better than he knew.[14] One should remember that Meyer said of Becket: "Ich habe diesen Charakter wirklich nicht gemacht, sondern er ist mir—in ungewöhnlichem Masse—erschienen."[15]

Meyer's Becket is many things; he is of contradictions all compact: a man of peace, gentle, pure in his private life, cultivated, humane; unable to bear the sight of blood, yet able, at need, to shed it with the best warriors of his sanguine century; merciful to animals and to deluded humans like a self-accused witch, yet merciless in his sublimated revenge on the King who has wronged him; cringingly humble, yet again arrogant with the assurance of being the wisest of mortals in a benighted age; incapable of violence, yet able to destroy King Henry's peace of soul by simply withdrawing his head from his councils and his hand from his sons; a frail and feminine person who yet at the end is transfigured in manliness; a victim of persecution who fears martyrdom yet courts it, and takes the death-blows with a smile of triumph, having punished his enemy by forcing the enemy to kill him and thus assure him of immortal sainthood. A follower of Christ who professes to serve Love but, in the opinion of Bertram de Born, is a better hater even than he; a saint and an astute diplomat, double-dealing with foreign kings yet innocent of any treason to his own king who has afflicted him; a politician who contrives to get himself elected by the English bishops as their head, but then turns into a true spiritual leader of the Church.

Various things in the story are left unclear; it was intended to be multivocal, "mehrdeutig," as Meyer wrote to Louise von François.[16] Did Becket bring pressure on the villainous Malherbe to release his victim Hilde? Did Becket spirit away the witch out of her cell? Why did Becket refuse Henry the kiss of reconciliation? This was seemingly a combination of aesthetic and ethical revulsions, but as Hans says—and his words might stand as a motto over much of the story: "Was in dem Innern des Kanzlers vorging, wer kann es sagen?" (165). Becket's face is like that of the Christ on the Schaffhausen painting, the eyes of which seem now closed, now open—"eine unehrliche Kunst," judges the Bowman (100). The very name of Becket's daughter, Gnade, introduces, no doubt designedly, a recurrent element of ambiguity, "weil Grazia wohl die himmlische Gnade bedeutet . . . aber ebensogut die feinste Blüte menschlicher Art und Anmut" (81). In the father's weird punning on the name, "schlimm, wenn die süsse Gnade verloren ging" (161), it has a triplicity of meanings: his own daughter, the royal favor he lost by turning against the King, and the heavenly grace Henry has forfeited through his misdeed. Hans says before he begins his story what we are ready to echo at its end: "O Herr, das sind schwere, unerforschliche Geschichten" (17). The events related, as the author himself remarks, are astounding and incomprehensible not only to the distant observer but to the immediate participants and reach down into depths of the soul where one's feeling becomes divided and one's thoughts stand as it were on the brink of an abyss (17). We seem to be face to face with the ultimate questionableness of all human motives and of life itself.[17]

By developing the legend about Thomas Becket's Saracen origin, Meyer has done most to add to the problematicalness of his hero. He himself wrote, in comment on his story: "der Dichter hat von dem orientalischen Ursprung des Thomas Becket Anlass genommen, demselben einen ganz eigentümlichen modernen Charakter zu geben, der mit dem mittelalterlich gewalttätigen des Königs notwendig in Kampf geraten muss" (*Bfe.* II, 99). By giving Becket this Oriental background, Meyer has made it possible to lodge in him antitheses which would be incompatible to the more logical Occidental mind: to be both cruel and kind, both vindictive and long-suffering, to pursue vengeance and to resign it to fate. Becket's inner world, as symbolized by his daughter and her setting, is Oriental in coloring; the fairytale-like "Waldschlösschen" with its Moorish architecture and its dark cypresses is an exotic enclave in the English forest. Becket speaks Arabic with his daughter, as he does later in addressing Christ: both belong for him to the Oriental world and are "imports" to the West. He has brought up his child without Christian forms, on Arabic lore,[18] and at her bier in the chapel there is no symbol of Christianity, only the figure of the father with torn hair and garments. The whole picture is so Eastern that it moves Hans to utter a verse from the Koran that he once read in Granada (89).

Meyer ascribes to the Saracen blood in both Thomas and Gnade their instinctive and unconditional subservience to royalty (74, 104). Thomas expressly warns Henry of this dangerous trait in himself, and admonishes him never to give him, his follower, into the hands of a more powerful lord (104). It is his nature to be the follower of a stronger one. He reminds Henry at the meeting on the heath: "Du kennst seit langem meine Natur, o Herr, die in den Stapfen eines Grösseren treten muss" (165). Previously he followed the King; now he is following the Nazarene. Long before this, however, Henry had recognized him for a Saracen unbeliever, "ein ungläubiger Philosoph und verkappter Sarazen" who took malicious pleasure in exposing the vices of the English clergy (94).

Fatalism, such as Hans reports the Arab astronomer in Granada as expounding (26), is in Thomas' Oriental blood. Even after the cruel wrong Henry has done him, he is willing to remain his Chancellor, for he believes "unsere Sterne und unsere Geburtsstunden stehen zu einander in Beziehung" (121). With the face and gesture of one who has sustained a mortal wound, he cries "Wohin werde ich geführt? In welchen Dienst und Gehorsam? In welchen Tod?" Yet a moment later, with a mixture of servility and fatalism, he assents: "Was du verhängst, das geschehe!" (122). When Henry marvels that Thomas did not denounce the traitor Fauconbridge earlier, Thomas refers to the "invisible arms" that move beneath every man's motions: "alles Ding kommt zur Reife und jeden ereilt zuletzt seine Stunde" (111)—words that contain a veiled foreboding of the King's own doom. "Schillernd," iridescent, like almost everything about

Thomas, this fatalism blends imperceptibly with Christian faith in God's eventual justice. Only later does Hans realize "dass der heimlich zu Tode Verwundete verdeckter und zweifelnder Weise von der dunkeln und langsamen Rache Gottes sprach" (105). At the end, Thomas will do nothing to save himself from the four murderers: let God's eternal decree *and* the King's will be done (183)!

As one of Oriental blood, as a sufferer and martyr, Thomas Becket feels himself a kinsman of Christ. When he differentiates between the corrupt body of the Church and its virtuous soul, he pretty clearly identifies himself with the latter and with "jener Andere" who personified its virtues (114). If Christ is the Other, then Becket himself, by inference, is the One, a brother and equal. Indeed, he calls himself "ein Diener und Bruder des Nazareners" (168). The more he himself suffers, the more he feels drawn to Christ, the "Prince of Suffering." Though he loves and follows Christ, he never refers to him by that name, and he never acknowledges His divinity: "ein Gott . . . , wie die Kirche lehrt," is as far as he goes (166). He speaks to the Crucified One lovingly and compassionately, as Hans overhears him, "but blasphemously and as to an equal" (107). He adores Him as a "himmlisches Gemüt"—which is not saying "ein Himmlischer"—but regards His martyrdom as having been in vain (107). He implores Christ's help to walk in His steps (which, on the other hand, would imply His being something more than human); he feels he belongs to Him and cannot leave Him, the long-suffering King of derided and crucified Humanity, "du geduldiger König der verhöhnten und gekreuzigten Menschheit" (108).

As the story progresses, the similarity with Christ is emphasized in external details: Thomas at the head of the flock of Saxon poor and oppressed; the sinner Queen Eleanore falling at his feet and venerating him as a saint; his triumphal progress, with branches and garments strewing his way, to Canterbury and martyrdom; his last supper with the company of his faithful, and his death with Christ's words on his lips. As the end nears, he addresses the Crucified One as "Fürst der Schmerzen," praying Him to enter his body, pierce his hands, and grant him His passion (187). Facing his murderers, he opens his arms wide, like the One on the cross above him, and utters His words: "Es geschehe!" (190). It is significant that Hans, as he recovers consciousness a few minutes later, for the first time refers to the slain man as "der Heilige" and shyly averts his gaze from him (191).

Becket's attitude toward Jesus as a great and admirable moral leader, human and not divine, is not incompatible with the attitude of a modern enlightened mind, perhaps with that of Meyer himself, though he is usually looked upon as an exemplar of orthodox Protestant Christianity. Meyer was conscious of being the child of a skeptical age; he wrote to his publisher Haessel: "ich habe ... Gottvertrauen (so viel ein Kind des XIX. Jahrhunderts haben kann)" (Bfe. II, 146). It is interesting to note that, though the figure or theme of Christ appears in the majority of his Novellen, Christ's divinity, debated in several of them, is not accepted beyond question until his very last work, *Angela Borgia* (1891).[19] There are other affinities, both obvious and concealed, between the author and his hero. To Louise von François, Meyer wrote: "Im Jenatsch und im Heiligen ... ist in den verschiedensten Verkleidungen weit mehr von mir, meinen wahren Leiden und Leidenschaften, als in dieser Lyrik, die kaum mehr als Spiel oder höchstens die Äusserung einer untergeordneten Seite meines Wesens ist."[20]

Adolf Frey, Meyer's friend and early biographer, said that he could hardly think of anyone more difficult to fathom than Meyer. He speaks of "Leidenschaftslosigkeit" as a fundamental trait of Meyer's nature; it was impossible to imagine him in a rage; "alles was fein, zart und tief ist, lebte in seiner Seele, aber die Kraft lebte nicht darin."[21] From his neurasthenic parents, Meyer had inherited refinement, but not vigor. Like Becket (and like Pescara) he knew he was suffering from a hidden wound that sapped his strength. He was aware of lacking, like Becket, "das Ungestüm und die Schärfe eines männlichen Blutes" (49). He knew Becket's pride of intellect, his scepticism and fatalism, his masquerading and make-believe. He even endows his hero with a brilliant verbal power like his own: Thomas can turn an offhand remark into a diplomatic speech, "dass es nur so strömte, wie flüssiges Gold" (48).[22] In Thomas Becket, Meyer has personified some of his own ambivalence, as he has the consciousness of his own frailty, indeed the frailty and questionableness of the life of the intellect such as he himself lived. In Becket, Meyer triumphs vicariously over the material world, the body and the over-sensitive nerves that have played him false;

but at the same time he casts doubt on the purity and unselfishness of that superior and fastidious Mind that resents the body's weaknesses. He sets a large question-mark after the "Saint."

The two chief characters in *Der Heilige* are diametrical opposites. Essentially they personify the spiritual and the physical natures of man: frail and problematical intellectuality opposed to robust and brutal vitality. Thomas is the man of thought and planning: self-contained, reticent, crafty, tenacious, and pliant; ready, as Saracen and Saxon, to subordinate himself, yet conscious of representing a superior civilization in a crude environment. Henry is the man of passion and action: impulsive, forthright, wilful in good and evil, naïvely immoral, a "Herrennatur" and a "blonde beast," given to blind rage and hatred, and therefore no match for his opponent's cold finesse and patience. The impotence of physical strength before the cool, quiet intelligence is drastically demonstrated in the scene where the Chancellor returns the seal of state (137). Against Becket's spiritual influence in the land, weapons are naught (141).

In the years of his chancellorship, Becket is the very incarnation of "Staatsweisheit" and devotion to the interests of his sovereign, including the tutelage of the four princes. He is Henry's brains. After losing the priceless aid of his counsel, the King commits one political blunder after another. As Richard says, his father quarrelled with Wisdom when he fell out with Becket (150). Previously, Richard had contrasted the two as a bristly boar and a fine Barbery steed (99). Other symbols are used for them: the Lion and the Snake, the Sun and the Moon. Henry, whom we first see with his eyes blazing like flames (41), suggests the sun, and, as we are soon reminded, "glänzende Sonnen gehen blutig unter" (44). Becket we first hear of in Cordova as Prinz Mondschein, so called because of the paleness and meekness of his countenance (28). The sun is masculine, the moon feminine;[23] the sun is passion and heart, the moon mind and head.

The mental principle triumphs in the end over the physical, refinement over vitality. Henry is driven to distraction by Thomas's spiritual tyranny, which preys upon him like a vampire (147). Even beyond the grave it pursues him, for he must needs revere Thomas as a saint and degrade himself by a shameful penance at his tomb (193f.). As Hans puts it, Henry finally collapses under the crushing weight of a holy corpse (193).

Between these two antagonists Meyer has set a figure of his own invention, Gnade, Becket's young daughter. She is made the chief factor in the motivation: the King's seduction of her, we are told, is what in the end costs him his crown, his life, and his soul's salvation (65). Clearly, the Gnade-action was in Meyer's eyes his chief contribution to the solution of the historical enigma of Thomas Becket. But did Meyer thereby lighten the darkness around Becket, or deepen it? Did he complicate his story by over-motivating, and in so doing exceed the slender proportions of the ideal Novelle? The real "Wendepunkt" is not Gnade's death—which is highly contrived—but the spiritual crisis induced in Thomas by his being made Archbishop of Canterbury. Accepting as he did the legend of the Saracen origin of his hero, the author might have contented himself with the problem—which is, *malgré lui*, his principal one—of the man of alien racial and religious provenience who is forced, for another's political interests but in accord with a deeper part of his own nature, into high religious office, and who resolves to take this office "seriously" and not as it was meant.[24] This alone is a stupendous problem and would have amply sufficed, without the somewhat sensational and trite motif of seduction.

The whole figure and episode of Gnade strike one as "erdacht" rather than truly "gesehen." She remains colorless and unconvincing in her relations to her father and to the King. She seems invented for a purpose, and is dropped as soon as that purpose has been served. Her scene with her father (76-79) is the weakest in the entire story: here Gnade and Thomas appear as the conventional figures of the pure and unsuspecting maiden and the fatuous father, and one is uneasily conscious of unassimilated literary antecedents in *Nathan der Weise* and *Emilia Galotti*.[25] The closing lines, with Thomas's words "Doch genug! Meine Stunde ist um ... Meinst du, dass ich dich liebe? Unermesslich! Mein Einziges, mein Alles!" and the kiss imprinted on her brow, are a lapse into *cliché*.

Gnade remains a symbol and an abstraction, not a flesh-and-blood girl like Keller's Vrenchen. Perhaps we can discern in these two figures a fundamental difference between the ways of the symbolist and the realist. Yet Meyer belongs indubitably to the period of Poetic Realism. We need only to compare his work with that of incipient Naturalism in Hauptmann's *Bahnwärter Thiel* to see that this is so. There is no woman figure in Meyer to compare even with Lene (and Naturalism was to go much further than that); the only really vulgar female in Meyer is Brigittchen von Trogen in *Plautus*, and he never ventured so far again.

Meyer's general attitude toward the world is that of a Poetic Realist. He said, according to his sister's record, "Jeder Gedanke muss seinen schönen Leib haben. Nur keine grauen Theorien. In der Poesie muss alles in Schönheit eingetaucht sein." Or again, "Poesie ist nicht Wahrheit, sie ist deren schöner Schein."[26] One can find typical passages of realism in *Der Heilige*, for example, in the opening pages, the setting and figures of a sharply observed, definite *locale;* the individuation in the women going to church, ending with the wrinkled, coughing old crones who have turned up their kirtles over their thin grey hair (7). Or again, in the final *milieu* of the story-telling session: the snoring dog by the fire, the gnawing mouse, the creaking lamp-chains (192). And in the whole account of the vicious and unpleasant situation summed up in the phrase "das unreife Kebsweib eines alten Königs" (83) there is more than a suggestion of modern realism.

Yet Meyer's historical predilection, and his conscious cultivation of style and symbol, make him a special case among the Poetic Realists. A realist should deal with the reality of his own time. Meyer comes no closer to the present than the 17th century. His heart, like that of the professor in Mann's *Unordnung und frühes Leid*, is with history as "happened," not as "happening." Meyer's historical sense is connected, consciously or subconsciously, with his cult of beauty and of death. Like Mann's hero, he is secretly on the side of the "eternalized" past, not the "lawless" present, of death, not life: "Das Vergangene ist verewigt, das heisst: es ist tot, und der Tod ist die Quelle aller Frömmigkeit und alles erhaltenden Sinnes."[27]

One may detect an implied criticism of contemporary realistic trends in the words he gives to his narrator: "Denn, Herr, es ist etwas anderes, wenn Könige und Heilige gegen einander fahren, als wenn in unseren schwäbischen Trinkstuben geschrien und gestochen wird" (18). This is a sort of reversal of Grillparzer's assertion of the significance of ordinary lives. It is also at variance with Keller's finding the great themes of the world's literature reappearing among his Swiss peasantry. Keller lovingly poeticized the near, the familiar and everyday. Meyer was an equally loyal Swiss, but his artistic home was not the present scene. Keller got his hands into the native soil before his door; Meyer fled from the "bürgerliche Gegenwart" to the great ages of the past. He confessed to Keller, "Ich muss mit der grossen Historie fahren."[28] Keller had noted—according to Meyer, half in praise and half in censure—Meyer's pronounced stylization, "mein starkes Stilisieren;" but Meyer declared it was in his blood (*Bfe.* I, 411).

As a stylist, Meyer required historical distancing and costuming. He wrote to Louise von François: "Am liebsten vertiefe ich mich in vergangene Zeiten, . . . die mir erlauben, das Ewig-Menschliche künstlerischer zu behandeln, als die brutale Aktualität zeitgenössischer Stoffe mir nicht gestatten würde."[29] His aristocratic nature felt repelled by everything common, petty, and vulgar; his nervous frailty made him instinctively shun the rough and tumble of the present and take refuge in the past. Frey quotes him as saying "Lange, lange war mir alles, was Wirklichkeit heisst, so zuwider als möglich."[30]

Meyer has been recognized as an historical realist, but perhaps one might best characterize him as a symbolical realist. He carries to its height the tendency toward symbolism which we have seen to be inherent both in the Novelle and in Poetic Realism. Things and persons in his works are sharply envisaged, but we feel that they are always meant to signify something beyond themselves. His style at its best blends realism and symbolism perfectly. Thus, for example, the amazing transformation in Becket is pointed up by the contrast between his courtier's feet clad in costly peaked-shoes (118) and the toes of his naked feet showing like yellow ivory beneath his dark, coarse hair shirt (128). We have already noted that the tendency toward symbolism is inherent in Poetic Realism; in Meyer it is simply developed more fully than in any other writer of this period.

Meyer likes to take for his symbol an object of art, such as the State Seal with the three leopards which the Chancellor returns to his sovereign, a "kostbares Gerät" of pure gold and precious stone. As it passes from Becket's hand, it symbolizes his withdrawal from the service of the King of England to enter that of a greater King whom he indicates by a mute gesture of his haggard arm heavenwards. Then the symbol is intensified: Henry, in consternation at his favorite's new aspect, lets the Seal fall to the marble floor ("es entglitt seiner Hand"—even as Thomas is doing), and when Hans picks it up he notes a fine crack running through the middle of the English arms—for the interests of the State are rent irreparably by the dissension of its brain and hand (133f.). In a later scene, Hans's heart rejoices over the amity between Richard and Thomas, and he forsees the end of the King's woes; but then, alas, he espies, perched on a pillar over the heads of the two, a horrid little stone monster that seems to mock all hope of reconciliation (163). In a fit of rage, again, Henry springs from his seat and knocks over his goblet, so that it rolls far over the banquet board, spilling red wine on the white linen like blood on snow (175)—an omen of the slaying of Becket, which Henry rashly incites to in his following words.

Sometimes the symbolism is subtly verbal, as when the words of the hymn intoned by the Saxons waiting for Thomas in the courtyard below are tacitly changed from the original "Vexilla Regis prodeunt" to "Vexilla Dei prodeunt" (137). Or the symbolism shades off into marked figurativeness: when the Chancellor obtained ameliorations for the oppressed Saxons, Hans says, he did not diminish the load of the beast of burden, only repacked it and saw to it that the thongs did not cut too deeply into the flesh (109). Becket's words, Hans avers, are graven into his grey head like the inscription on an overturned Roman milestone, even fragments of which still bear the indelibly cut characters (116).

In *Der Heilige* the background of Nature is sparingly used. On the whole, it is conventional and devoid of local color, save for the Zürich details in the brief opening picture. Meyer knew little of the French countryside, and that of England was completely unfamiliar to him. We have the traditional motif of the storm that disperses a hunting party, and the "getreuer Eckhart" figure of the trusty retainer who finds shelter and egress for his king from a tangled wood in which they were lost (59f.). At other times, however, Nature takes on a symbolic value or "Stimmungswert." Autumn sets the stage of impending evil (68). A clouded crescent moon (as in the final scene of Wallenstein's life) casts a fitful light upon dire doings (83). Bare boughs hang low and black as if in mourning as Hans and Äscher flee after Gnade's death (84). "Das Welken und Sterben der Natur" sets the key for the ill-starred attempt at reconciliation (160). Becket and the King meet "an einem grauen Tage und auf einer trübseligen Heide" in northern France (164). After the dismal failure of the meeting, the autumnal mood is deepened, with raw winds and the first flakes of snow. Then the snowfall thickens, gloomy birds swoop overhead; autumn has passed into winter (171f.).

All his life, Meyer nursed dramatic ambitions, and all his Novellen, he testified, were originally conceived in dramatic form.[31] Perhaps one obstacle in the way of dramatization was his instinctive need for "distancing" his matter, which was incompatible with the immediacy of stage action. As a matter of fact, most of his stories are told in the third person, not the direct "ich-Form," and gain a further remove through their frame. Be that as it may, Meyer's case is another proof of the kinship between drama and Novelle. Though he had to resign the attempt to build plays, he had something of the capacity of the playwright: he saw, plastically, scenes and figures in motion. Posture and gesture are marked all through his story, and there is indeed a "dramatischer Gang" and "dramatischer Stoss" in it, as he claimed (*Bfe*. II, 306, 90). The crucial dispute between King and Chancellor (130-138) is dramatically envisaged, with impressive contrast between the violent words and movements of the one and the quiet speech and inactivity of the other. Equally dramatic, though brief, is our last glimpse of the dying ruler: his hand outstretched in forced blessing over his son, but distorted into a gesture more like a curse as the fatal stroke overtakes it in midair (204).

Some of Meyer's scenes, however, are devoid of dramatic movement and are purely pictorial or even sculptural. The final scene of martyrdom on the altar steps, though climactically "built up," ends with the picture of the saint's dying face, seen in narrowed focus as the narrator loses consciousness (190). And perhaps the finest of all the scenes in the story is completely static: the exquisite picture of the dead Gnade lying in the little chapel of her Moorish castle in all her exotic beauty amid a colorful and fairytale setting; and beside her face, even more dead-looking, that of her father—one feels the hand of the sculptor in this motionless, soundless representation of Beauty and Death (88f.).

Meyer ties his tale together, as it were, with bridges of anticipation and realization: early events prefigure later ones, omens are fulfilled, themes are echoed. Becket's experiences at the court of Cordova are a prefiguration of his later ones at the court of London, and both eventuate in bloody violence. The fate of the Saxon Hilde foreshadows that of Becket's own daughter; in both cases a rapacious Norman preys upon a defenseless girl of the "inferior" race; and later events bring out the tragic irony in the words which Hilde's despairing father flings after the elegant churchman: "Schade, Pfaffe, dass du kein Kind hast, das dir ein Normanne verderben kann!" (39). There is a suspense value, as well as medieval color, in the vision of a prophetic nun who sees a white lily, signifying a saint, sprouting from the marriage bed of Gilbert Becket and a Saracen woman (32). Thomas's conversation with Hans about Christ's kissing Judas (108) prepares for his later refusal to kiss the King in reconciliation (166). His championship of the witch prepares for his subsequent championship of the Saxons. Rollo's reference to the "böses Sterben" of the Norman kings prepares us for Henry's end. When Becket, the first time he talks to Hans, says "Ich liebe das Denken und die Kunst und mag es leiden, wenn der Verstand über die Faust den Sieg davonträgt und der Schwächere den Stärkeren aus der Ferne trifft und überwindet" (42f.), he anticipates our later knowledge of him and the further course of the action. Becket's warning to the King, "Gib mich nie aus deiner Hand in die Hand eines Herrn, der mächtiger wäre, als du!" (104) is echoed later (122, 133), after Henry has disregarded the warning. Like the author of the *Nibelungenlied* in the prophetic fourth line of his stanzas, Hans frequently sounds the note of coming doom and thereby creates suspense. As Gnade receives her death-wound in Hans's arms, so does her father, and Hans is spattered with the victims' blood. The closed eyes and exultant smile of Becket's dying face have been curiously prefigured by the face of Chorherr Burkhard at the beginning of the story (190, 11). The Crossbowman quits the King's service in the very room in which he entered it, under vastly different auspices (199), and he effectively terminates his tale by falling to his knees and echoing his remorseful plaint of twenty-one years ago: "Mea culpa, mea maxima culpa!" (191f.).

Another compositional device by which Meyer knits his narrative more closely is that of the leitmotif, which is of course related to the symbol. The story is told by a crossbowman, so it is natural that we have a "cluster" of symbols such as bow, string, bolt, and arrow. Even the detail of young Hans's cutting an arrow-straight line through the great "bow" of the Rhine seems to be in character (22). The bolt that killed William Rufus is the chief "exhibit" in the brief scene in the armory with Rollo (44). The tensing of a bowstring (83) is the prelude to Gnade's death by an arrow from her own battlements. A terrible glance of Becket's strikes Hans with the force of a bolt (90). Becket's defection is likened to the wounding of Henry's heart by a poisoned arrow (138). Distances are measured in bowshots (164).

An individual leitmotif is used for characterization in the case of Gui Malherbe. This predatory Norman has swooped down like a bird of prey and carried off a Saxon girl in her father's absence (38). Then we see him, on a similar adventure, showing in profile "den scharfen Haken seines Raubvogelgesichtes" (68). And Henry, warned, resolves to abduct his paramour "bevor der Habicht die Taube zerfleischt" (69). The big Saxon Trustan Grimm is marked on his first appearance by his red hair (40), and each time he reappears, this motif is repeated.

Perhaps the most prominent characterizing motif is that of the eye. Becket's dark eyes with their hidden depths, usually lowered as if to conceal his thoughts and feelings, are noted very early in the story, where he is described as barely glancing at a suppliant "mit einem dunkeln Blicke aus seinen halbgeschlossenen Augen" (39). Again and again it is said of him that he casts down his dark eyes; they can also be "vorwurfsvoll," with the fires of grief and hatred in their depths (90) and "tief schmerzlich," seeming to look more inward than outward (159); finally they become "strahlend" with the light of beginning transfiguration (169). Gnade has her father's "dunkle, schwermütige Augen" (71).

Of King Henry, on the other hand, when he first appears, it is said "seine blauen unbeschatteten Augen brannten wie zwei Flammen" (41). His eyes are "leuchtend" (63), and "lusttrunken" while Gnade's are "flehend und furchtsam" (70). With "freudestrahlende Augen" he is ready to bestow the Primacy on Becket (117); but later he glares in anger with flashing blue eyes that seem about to start from his head (137, 195). "Mit rollenden Augen" he berates his Normans (176).

Richard has his father's "grosse blaue Augen" (98), which

shine in happy confidence of the reconciliation of Becket and the King (151). Hans himself has "funkelnde Augen" (17); the Saxon maiden Hilde, who is for him "die Freude und der Wunsch meiner Augen" (37), has "tiefliegende blaue Augen" (200) which become "strahlend" just before she dies (201). Equally characterizing are Malherbe's "unruhige Augen" (39), the "schwarze, irre Augen" of the alleged witch (53), the "unstete, beschäftigte Augen" of the Queen (54), the guilty Äscher's "hilflose, matte" (80) and Monna Lisa's "von Tränen gerötete Augen" (87), and the "brennende Augen" of the Saxon mother (144) and of Bertram de Born (153).

The note of "Gnade" or Grace runs in various modulations all through Meyer's composition. The London clergy, we are told, took care to convert the Saracen princess before they would permit her to marry Gilbert Becket. They might conceivably have baptized her Fidelitas, for she had faithfully sought the man she loved over half the earth. But they chose to call her Grazia or Grace—"um der grossen Gnade willen, welche die Mutter Gottes der Ungläubigen erwiesen!", as Meyer (rather than Hans) adds ironically (32). Thus the author introduces—for his source gave the name as Mathilda—that pervasive ambiguity which we have already noted. Aside from those "clusters" of equivocation (81, 161), the word occurs in a variety of meanings: as a title (Eure Gnade, 42), as preferments at Court (Gnaden, 43), as favor (Becket looking "gnädig" upon Hans, 46), as royal favor, proffered by the sovereign adventurer to the unknown lady of the woodland manor (62), or to be heaped upon the bereaved father after her death (86). It has the force of royal dignity (130) and of divine grace (32, 157). The memory of Gnade, the innocent girl, intervenes as a psychical "block" at the last moment to prevent Becket from exchanging the kiss of peace with her violator (165). Her name, and his smoldering grudge over her loss, are first clearly avowed a moment later (166), and this draws from Henry in turn a curse upon Gnade and the open charge of vengefulness against Thomas (169). It is surely no accident that the four murderers make for Le Havre, "dem ... Seehafen, welchen sie den Port der Gnade nennen" (179), or that when all is over, Hans is "abgegnadet" (for the more usual "abgedankt") and dismissed from the service of his sovereign (199).

With Thomas is associated the motif of the moon, gentle and cool and pale. He first enters the story as "Prinz Mondschein," the hero of a pretty Moorish fable (28); his rapt and kindly countenance shines like the moon (66); his benign influence stands over the grieving Saxons "wie der Vollmond in der Nacht" (144). With this moon-character the serene calm of "der ewig Ruhige" (47) seems to accord. Time is measured by the moon (64). The crescent moon has a Saracen suggestion (67, 83). The moon, coming out of the clouds, reveals the fugitives and brings death to Gnade (83). This whole scene is linked with the moonlight, and when in a "mondhelle Lichtung" a light-colored deer causes Äscher's horse to shy and kill him, we feel a weird suggestion of Becket's supernatural influence punishing his faithless servant (84f.).

With the motif of the moon is linked the trait of pallor which we note in Becket's "farbloses Antlitz" when we first see him (37) and which is consistently repeated: "ein ... bleicher Mann" (42); "noch blasser als sonst" (47); "farblose Lippen" (49); "totenblass" (50); "die blassen Züge" (66); "der Blasse" (67). His pale face blanches to complete colorlessness at the King's proposal (118), but he finally bows "sein bleiches Haupt" in submission (122). Rollo condemns him for a "blasse Memme" (125). His bare feet beneath his sackcloth show the characteristic pallor (128). This color is transferred to the snake that becomes another symbol for Becket: "dieser sonnte sich, wie eine schlanke weisse Schlange, in den Strahlen der fürstlichen Gunst" (48). That Becket habitually rides a white palfrey seems to comport with his general note of pallor and gentleness. Ironically, the pale cast of Becket's features finally infects the King's: the "matte, weisse Schein" of Henry's face, according to Rollo, reflects the pallor of "der Bleiche," "das Pfaffengesicht," "die Schlange" which stabs him from underground with its poisonous fangs (197).

The "Blässemotiv" passes over into the "Todesmotiv." The pale Becket by Gnade's coffin is marked by death (100); he sits like a dead man at the King's table (101); he conceals, like Pescara, a mortal wound (105). He remonstrates, with the face of one dying, against his elevation to the Primacy; he feels himself led thereby into death (122). The symbolism of Beauty and Death connected with Gnade is picked up again, with Meyer's characteristic fondness for objects of art, in the ancient marble dug up in the Roman square at Arles: a girl's head with broken eyes and the bitterness of death upon its lips and writhing adders for hair (156). To Bertram's band, it foretells "ein kommendes grosses Sterben" to be visited upon their sunny land. To Herr Burkhard, the man of the Church, it signifies the blight of heresy, which must be extirpated (157). In either case, Death will be the victor, as it so often is in Meyer's poetic world.

CHAPTER NINE

STORM, *DER SCHIMMELREITER* (1888)

The last and longest of Theodor Storm's fifty-odd Novellen, *Der Schimmelreiter*, may be regarded as his masterpiece. Under the stress of experience, especially private sorrow, Storm's art matured and deepened toward the end of his life. The writer of soft, sentimental idylls, perfumed with faded flowers and blurred by hopeless reminiscence, became a tragic poet who coped, in strong, sharp-lined, cogent Novellen, with the bitter realities of life. Among these later works again, one can observe both a deepening and a simplification. From the historical remoteness of the "Chroniknovellen," the stylized "Minnewelt" of *Ein Fest auf Haderslevhuus* or the artificial archaism of *Aquis Submersus*, the *Schimmelreiter* at length comes home to treat, unsentimentally and in timeless terms, the tragedy of a modern man.

Two of Storm's most characteristic tendencies reach perfection in his final work: his "Stimmungskunst," no longer an end in itself or a lyrical self-indulgence, as in his early tales, but creating the atmosphere and background for vigorous action; and his "Heimatkunst," which limited itself to the small patch of the world that he knew well, but within these limits plumbed ultimate depths. The fate of a great individual is here closely interwoven with the character and fate of his race and region, which are Storm's own. No other work of his, I believe, unites, so maturely developed, so many idiosyncrasies of his style and his *Weltanschauung*.

In place of the frail, passive heroes and heroines of Storm's earlier tales, who end in wistful resignation and whose fate evokes in us pathetic rather than tragic emotions, we meet in the later Novellen more resistant protagonists. Yet even in *Aquis Submersus* much still depends on accident and the conditions of a period; beneath the astringent realism of *Hans und Heinz Kirch* there is still a residue of the sentimental tragedy of misunderstanding; and for lack of a real antagonist in the son, *Carsten Curator* remains merely harrowing. Not until *Der Schimmelreiter* do we get the full-fledged "Willensmensch," a formidable champion who confronts the present and the future with clear eye, instead of dreamily ruminating the past. Hauke

Haien is the peer of the great forces that oppose him, and his fate is commensurate with his nature and his ambition. He wills his great work: "Ich will," he declares, and repeats, "ich will, dass das grosse Vorland . . . eingedeicht werde."[1] And when life has lost its value for him, he wills his own death.

Der Schimmelreiter celebrates the creative individual, the man with a dream and a mission, the genius—opposed, with almost Hebbelian antithesis, to the dull, levelling "Masse." Hauke stands head and shoulders above his fellows (376); he acts for their interest against their opposition; when once he invites their cooperation, they tangle his feet in petty compromises (330); when he takes their shortsighted advice (359f.) it is a sign of the impairment of his personality and it proves his undoing. Loneliness is the inevitable lot of such a man, an intensification of the "fürchterliche Einsamkeit" which Storm saw to be the fate of all human beings.[2] Finally, he cannot confide even in his wife, his only comrade; he is starkly alone with his guilt and his remorse.

For the factor of personal guilt is by no means ruled out; Hauke is not simply the hapless victim of a world that, Schiller tells us, "liebt . . . das Strahlende zu schwärzen / Und das Erhabne in den Staub zu ziehn." It has been alleged, to be sure, that Schiller's concept of guilt and atonement, "Schuld und Sühne," is virtually absent from Storm's works. Storm himself expressly rejected the older view of tragedy resulting from "eine spezielle *eigene* Schuld des Helden" as too narrow and juristic, and advocated a deterministic view that recognized "die Schuld des Allgemeinen," the guilt of the age, the social class, the heredity[3] and environment in which we participate and which we are powerless to oppose.[4] But, however great a share of responsibility he assigns to the "unpropitious stars" of circumstance, Storm exposes clearly the tragic flaw in his hero.

We should not overrate the importance of the closing words of the Schoolmaster (376) when he aligns Hauke Haien with Socrates and Christ as one of those spiritual leaders whom humanity has "ever crucified and burned." This shrewd little rationalist, sickly, deformed, "entgleist," has special grounds for being critical of society and his mental inferiors and for championing the "Aufklärer" in Hauke. If we look back over his narrative, however, we shall find, consistently developed, other traits in the hero that combine to motivate the tragic outcome.

Storm's art of character-drawing is seen at its height in *Der Schimmelreiter*. Whereas in the early stories the figures are typical and insufficiently individuated, in *Der Schimmelreiter* the typical and the individual, the symbolic and the realistic, are admirably blended. Even incidental persons are distinctly outlined with a few firm strokes. What a vivid picture we get, at the start, of the narrator, with his threadbare black coat, his thin grey hair and black lashes over bright eyes, his delicate features and plaintive voice, his hunched shoulder, his superior smile!

Upon his hero, Storm throws light from many sides: we see him as a tender husband and father and as an unrelenting driver of himself and others; we see him in his profound if unconventional religiousness, his tolerance, his humility before an inscrutable God, his mercifulness toward animals and harshness toward human sloth and superstition, his growing avidity for land and power; —and all these traits are manifested, not through direct description, but through action, even in minor gestures.

Der Schimmelreiter, in short, proves once more the ability of the Novelle to give a full-length portrait of a hero. Storm does not restrict himself to illuminating only a crucial experience in the life of an already developed character, but shows us all the chief stages and conditioning factors in his hero's development from boyhood to maturity and death. Yet, for all the wealth of characterizing incident, there is one central "Ereignis" and conflict around which everything is built with the close-knit structure that distinguishes the Novelle. The "Wendepunkt," almost exactly midway in the story, is the hero's resolve to build his new type of dike.

The goal is clear from the beginning, and this circular movement or analytic procedure, which makes a "frame" seem appropriate, may perhaps be regarded as implicit in the Novelle, in distinction from the novel, which normally begins without such "Zielsetzung." In the present case, we start with an extraordinary phenomenon, a specter, and by the end know how it came to be. So in *Kasperl und Annerl*, in *Der arme Spielmann*, and in Otto Ludwig's *Zwischen Himmel und Erde*, we get first the present situation and then the action that produced it; and so Kleist "gives away" the end of *Michael Kohlhaas* in his opening paragraph. In *Die Marquise von O . . .* and in *Das Erdbeben in Chili*, likewise, Kleist starts with an arresting and paradoxical state of affairs which the plot, by returning into the past, is to elucidate and develop.

In *Der Schimmelreiter*, Storm gives us an uncommonly complete picture of a lifetime, and takes pains to show already in the child the qualities that will mark the man for better and worse. We see the solitary boy spending his days on the dike, intently studying the ways of the water, defying the sea devils, conceiving the ideal of the novel dike that is to be his life-work. We note his independent and critical mind that challenges the accepted, his enterprise and persistence, his withdrawal from his fellows as he sits on his overturned wheelbarrow, studying (259). We also see the hardness in his nature come out in his stoning of birds and his savage reprisals on the big cat (265f.). The sharpness and impatience that later make him so unpopular with his easygoing fellows appear in his angry shout to the noisy waves: "Ihr könnt nichts Rechtes, sowie die Menschen auch nichts können!" (261)—a challenge to the two powers that are to be the great adversaries of his life. Much later, at the zenith of his success, we shall see him, in statuesque and symbolic pose, on his dike, dominating for a space these two enemies: the storm-whipped sea on one side and reluctant men, bending to his iron will, on the other (341). The concluding frame reintroduces these two as the final victors: the dull mass, essentially unchanged since Hauke's time, and the treacherous sea, still destructive beneath its smiling surface (375-377).

The aspiration to become Dikegrave early takes shape in the boy's mind (260f.). The stripling hears himself called the virtual official, and ambition begins to brood in his young head (284). With the last words of his dying father, which are a sort of spiritual legacy (299),[5] this latent ambition grows apace and soon shows signs of *hybris*. He tells himself "mehr als zu oft" that he is the man for the office; he nurses a resentment for the people he imagines contesting his rightful claim. These thoughts obsess him, "und so wuchsen in seinem jungen Herzen neben der Ehrenhaftigkeit und Liebe auch die Ehrsucht und der Hass" (299). He is right in regarding himself as the best man for the job, and his novel dike ultimately proves its worth. But in the pursuit of a just cause he warps his soul; he is eventually ruined, like Kleist's Kohlhaas, by excess in his chief virtue, which is the most poignant kind of tragedy.

The ideal of dike reform goes back to his boyhood, but the particular project in which he applies it is undertaken under mental compulsion, as compensation for a sense of inferiority: "Sie sollen nicht mehr sagen, dass ich nur Deichgraf bin von meines Weibes wegen!" (309). He, the clear-headed, intellectually honest man, is untrue to himself in acting under the whip of emotion. When his wife asks him "Hast du denn guten Mut dazu?", he answers with telltale haste "Das hab ich" (312). We think of Cangrande's dictum in Meyer's *Die Hochzeit des Mönchs*: "Wer gestossen wird, springt schlecht."

Increasing opposition isolates Hauke and begets defiance and secretiveness in his heart. His personality splits: toward workmen and servants he grows unsparingly harsh; toward his wife alone he is tender, and his child he worships "als sei dort die Stätte seines ewigen Heils" (338). Vindicated at last by his superiors, exulting to hear his name given to the new-won land, he rises in the saddle and proudly surveys his domain. In his mind, his dike takes on the proportions of an "achtes Weltwunder," he sees himself towering above all other Frisians and looking sharply and pityingly down on them (346)—this is such vaunting as calls down the vengeance of the gods.

A nearly fatal illness leaves him physically weak, and a weariness of the spirit comes over him—"und wahrlich, es geht keine Müdigkeit über die des Starken und Tapfern," as the old Ritter von Glaubigern observes in Raabe's *Schüdderump*, he too grown weary in fighting a hostile world. At a critical moment, Hauke compromises for the sake of peace (360), and in the end he must face God with the heartbroken avowal "Ich habe meines Amtes schlecht gewartet" (373).

There is a certain similarity between Hauke Haien and the Faust of Part Two. Hauke too takes up the fight with the "senseless" ocean and wrests land from it, with the Devil allegedly helping him—though actually Hauke stands, as the aged Faust would, before Nature "ein Mann allein." He too is a benefactor of humanity, though his procedure is sometimes tyrannical. He too is sure that the traces of his earthly days cannot in aeons perish. Conversely to Faust, he meets disaster by ceasing to strive, by lying down for one fatal instant on the "Faulbett" of compromise. And for him there is no final salvation and assumption into Heaven, despite all labor and love; his end, like that of all living creatures in Storm's view, is utter extinction.[6]

Death's sombre note is struck early and often in *Der Schimmelreiter*. The blackened corpses washed up by the sea, the killing of birds and the cat by Hauke, the death of his father and of Elke's, each casting its shadow before and after, the broad space given to the funeral, the drowning of Trin Jans's son, and her own death, surrounded with weird foreboding, that ushers in the final act of this drama—at every turn we are reminded of "de Dod, de allens fritt" (301). Out of the hands of two dead, as it were, Hauke receives the land that is the first stepping-stone to his ambition (295), and another death enables him to marry (301). Even from the peaceful Marsch we hear the lowing of frightened cattle and the shrill scream of a lark being devoured (325)—a far cry indeed from the Romantic bird of Storm's earlier work. And yet this very theme of transiency and death proves, more clearly than anything else, how far Storm's literary roots reach back into the "Nachtseite" of Romanticism.

Inorganic nature is seen as a blind, pernicious force. The sea crumbles the dikes and drowns men and sheep, and on its shore little Wienke stands, a pathetic representative of humanity, petrified with terror, staring into the abyss, "den Abgrund, darin das Nichts" (356; cf. I, 109). Nature is hostile to man, even when it seems friendliest (360). All its destructive fury centers at last upon the hero (368), and in an uproar of "Weltuntergangsmusik," through which cuts the cry of a gull trampled to death, "die Nacht, der Tod, das Nichts" engulf the world (370). But after its orgy of destruction, unfeeling Nature smiles again "im goldensten Sonnenlichte" (377), just as, at the close of *Haderslevhuus*, the stars look down in imperturbable calm on human anguish (VII, 72).

Profundity and cogency of tragic thought are matched in this story by high excellence of form. The threefold "frame" has been criticized as artificial, and to be sure the outer frame is not completed: we do not return at the end to the young reader of the magazine story; we do return to the "middle-frame" narrator, the Traveller, but the story proper is told by the "inner-frame" narrator, the Schoolmaster. A frame is in any case an artifice, a device for distancing and objectifying which Storm's lyrical, subjective genius found especially useful and which he developed to mastery, though never to such elaborateness as Meyer. Here, the triple depth seems appropriate to the scope and significance of the story, like a rich, graduated frame leading the eye inward to an impressive painting.

The frame is reintroduced as the Schoolmaster from time to time interrupts his account. These interruptions are by no means arbitrary, but are a structural element. The first one (264) marks the close of the first chapter of the hero's life, and the opening of the next with the words "da wurde es auf einmal anders mit ihm." Furthermore, this interruption has a "Stimmungswert," a musical value: it sounds again the initial leitmotif of the ghostly rider and deepens the mood of mystery that has just been induced by the incident of the "Norwegian sea-devils." The second interruption reintroduces the Schimmelreiter, and again we hear an echo of the original motif: the Rider and his pale horse plunge once more into the mere (297).

Most of the listeners now leave, the circle narrows to the Traveller and the Schoolmaster, and as the locale shifts to the intimacy of the latter's room, the narrative also becomes deeper, more analytical and complex (298). The next time the Schoolmaster breaks into his tale, it is for the purpose of drawing a sharp line between the data he himself has collected and the superstitious talk of the village which he must now introduce (314f.); here again, therefore, the interruption makes an artistic partition in the matter. The last break (362) similarly serves to distinguish the natural from the supernatural: the facts of Hauke's weakness and remorse on the one hand, and Trin's dying vision and the portents from Heaven on the other. This sets the stage and furnishes the historical-legendary background for the final climactic scenes. If one notes the location of these interruptions, moreover, one recognizes an approximate symmetry in their distribution.

It has been objected that, in a style as realistic as that of *Der Schimmelreiter*, the intrusion of the supernatural is inconsistent and obscuring. Storm doubtless had a racial and personal predilection for the ghostly, and it figures in several of his stories, most specifically in *Bulemanns Haus* and *Am*

Kamin. He himself remarked that any residual unclearness in his *Schimmelreiter* was due to the fact "dass ich einen sagenhaften Stoff ins rein Menschliche hinübergezogen habe."[7] At the same time he was unwilling to divest his hero of all his spectral attributes. In fact he declared it to be his intention "eine Deichgespenstsage auf die vier Beine einer Novelle zu stellen, ohne den Charakter des Unheimlichen zu verwischen," and the latter part of the story was to show the transformation of a man into a phantom.[8] For Storm, clearly, as for other Novelle-writers, a "fringe" of the supernatural and inexplicable was not incompatible with realism, but rather a legitimate part of the picture of life.

One cannot maintain, as Storm's most recent editor does, that the ghostly element has no deeper meaning here than that of an artistic expedient, and that the content of the story is simply the tragedy of a superior individual wrecked by the hostility and incomprehension of his fellow-men.[9] The supernatural is given more than artistic or "atmospheric" reality: it is indubitably objectified. At the very beginning, the Traveller, who gives every impression of being a rational man, and who as yet knows nothing of the legend, clearly sees the soundless Rider in his characteristic action (253f.).[10] Later, from the inn window, he again sees the apparition rush by, and even the Schoolmaster, bidden to pause, seems to imply its existence when he remarks seriously "Ihr braucht Euch nicht zu fürchten; ich hab ihn nicht geschmäht" (264). In the concluding "frame," the present dikegrave challenges the opinions of the "enlightened" and reminds the Traveller that he saw the specter with his own eyes. And the Traveller can only shrug his shoulders and evade a decision by saying "das muss beschlafen werden" (377).

How real, one may ask, is the white horse that is alleged to materialize out of the bleached bones on the island? Who is the Slovak with the clawlike hand who sells it to Hauke and laughs like a fiend after him (323)? The fact that this episode is reported by the clear-headed Hauke lends it a disconcerting factuality. Daylight realism, as in Kleist's *Kohlhaas*, shades off into the dubious twilight of the occult.[11] Again, the instant improvement in Elke's critical condition suggests a supernatural efficacy in Hauke's "unholy" prayer (336). The gift of "second sight," which the Frisians, according to Storm, share with the Scots, seems to manifest itself in Tede Haien as he gazes "wie abwesend" into his son's face, reading his future (260, 269). There is a note of doom forewrit, also, in the theme of the "foundation sacrifice:" the enlightened Hauke prevents the immuring of a stray dog, but in the end throws himself and his horse into the breach in the dike, which thenceforth holds.

This injection of the supernatural is not to be taken as an inartistic equivocation on Storm's part, but as integral with his *Weltanschauung* as revealed in this story. Storm, like Annette von Droste-Hülshoff, was fairly haunted by a dread of the Unknown and Unknowable that lurks outside our reasoned world, ready at all times to invade it. When he received the happy news that ended his long years of exile, he looked around in the circle of his family and asked which of them must now be sacrificed. The death of his wife soon answered his gloomy question. The very eyes of Storm's portraits seem to betray this deep-set apprehension.

His hero's whole life is an effort to build a secure rampart against the fearsome Infinite symbolized by the sea, to hedge off and preserve a clear realm of reason against the encroaching dark of the incomprehensible. Hauke's strong dike delimits his life and shelters it and his loved ones and the community of which he is the leader. But as the sea forever gnaws at the dike, so are man's defenses continually being broken down, and the battle-line between the natural and the supernatural is but a "fluid front."

The dike provides a dramatic unity of place and action. It is the elevated stage over which the chief events pass, with different lighting and different actors from the lone individual to masses manipulated with surprisingly modern technique. There is a definitely dramatic quality in the brief, sharply outlined scenes of which the story is composed, with a minimum of connecting narration and psychological analysis.[12] We do not get an unbroken continuum, but a spotlighting of decisive happenings, with "Gedankenstriche" to mark the intervals. Such a scene as that of the building of the dike in the teeth of an autumn storm (340ff.), with its movement of individuals and groups, its striking sound-effects, its emotional tension, is an eminently dramatic performance. Other scenes, again, are of a statuesque and symbolic kind: Elke standing, shading her eyes, looking anxiously after husband and child as they ride off to sea in a rising storm, while old Trin sits by, a norn-like figure, muttering incomprehensible prophecy with her withered lips (350). There is a masterly combination of realism and mystery in the short scene of Trin's death, down to the last touch of the creaking bedstead (362f.).

Storm shows an unusual power of dramatic visualization. He sees his persons in motion, and speech is regularly accompanied by dramatic gesture. The deliberate Tede Haien twists himself a chew of tobacco and stows it away in his mouth before answering (260); he shifts his quid meditatively, and, as he talks, strides up and down, emitting the black juice (270). Trin stands panting before him, prodding her crooked stick into the ground, flashing her keen eyes at him (267), or nodding her long nose mournfully over her dead cat and wiping her watering eyes with gout-twisted hand (268). The concluding paragraph of this interview is a fine piece of realistic "business" (269).

Elke is first seen in natural pose beside her house door, one hand behind her grasping a ring in the wall; she lets it fall with a clang as she speaks (271). The Pastorin lays down her fork in open-mouthed amazement (300); the puzzled Oberdeichgraf rubs his forehead (306); Hauke impatiently kicks a stone across the street (283)—one could enumerate many examples of such vivifying "business" accompanying speech. We are again reminded of the obbligato of gesture and movement in the Novellen of Kleist, the dramatist. That Storm was conscious of some dramatic capacity in himself is indicated by his remark, on finishing *Der Schimmelreiter*, that if he were ten years younger he would undertake the writing of drama. And we know that he ranked the Novelle as the sister and, for his time, the successor of great drama (VIII, 122f.).

The dialogue in *Der Schimmelreiter* is notably terse. These Northern natures prize brevity and understatement. They make few words and fall silent, relying on a gesture, a glance, or the other's intuition to supply the unsaid. The colloquies between father and son are masterpieces of laconism, the more impressive for a dozen lines of unprecedented eloquence on Tede's part (270) which, one feels, are the unburdening of years of silent observation. Throughout, the scenes that contain the most emotion are the most restrained in utterance; especially the meetings of the young lovers. Storm has demonstrated his great art of saying much with a few words that vibrate with overtones.

Sounds, on the other hand, are lavishly employed: sounds of the water, from the soft rustle of the incoming tide to the pounding of the storm-driven surf; sounds of the wind, from summer breezes to hurricane; animal notes, such as the lowing of cattle, the cries of waterfowl or warbling of larks; or the convivial noises of banqueting, the shouting of angry men above the storm —all these and many more make up the rich "sound-track" of this story. The absence of sound, especially in the movements of the spectral horse on island and dike, gives an uncanny effect.

The scene of the completing of the dike (341-344) re-echoes with sounds: "das Geklatsch des Regens ... das Brausen des Windes ... die scharfen Befehlsworte ... Männer schrien ... das Getöse des Wetters ... das Geräusch der Arbeiter, das Klatschen der hineingestürzten Kleimassen, das Rasseln der Karren und das Rauschen des Strohes ... das Winseln eines Hundes ... ein jammervoller Schrei ... eine rauhe Stimme von unten herauf"—all this in one page of print. Throughout the final scenes, again (365-375), sounds are prominent: the rattling of windows and shutters in the growing tempest, the tinkling of shattered glass, the creaking of beams, the rustling of the old ash tree, the ceaseless roar of wind and waves, and on this background, as solo voices, the plaintive call of a terrified child, the barking of a dog, the screech of a dying gull, the trumpet-like neighing of the white horse charging off as to battle. Finally the sound reaches an overwhelming crescendo: "der Sturm setzte nicht mehr aus; es tönte und donnerte, als solle die ganze Welt in ungeheurem Hall und Schall zugrunde gehen" (368); "ein Brausen wie vom Weltuntergang füllte ihre Ohren und liess keinen anderen Laut hinein" (374). With the thunder of the seas rushing through the breach, the cry of a despairing man, the scream of a horse forced to plunge to its death, this mighty storm-symphony comes to a close.[13]

It is by no means inapt to speak of Storm's work in such musical terms. His personal relation to music was exceptionally close all through his life, and as a writer both in prose and verse he wrought with an awareness of musical values and laws. "Stimmung," essentially a musical element, is one of the most characteristic features of his production. In his early "Stimmungsnovellen," in fact, it is the dominant and cohesive element in a loosely-strung series of pictures. In his later "Konfliktnovellen" it is subordinated to the action, but by no means eliminated.

Storm said of himself "ich arbeite meine Prose wie Verse." In this conscious artistry, which increased in the latter part of his career, the musical value of his language became an important consideration; there is evidence that he "heard" what he wrote. He grew more and more sensitive to the rhythm of his sentences, as Köster has pointed out; a multitude of inconspicuous alterations proves this. His fine discrimination between the rhythms of verse and prose led him to excise rigorously the iambic pentameters that had crept into the first version of *Haderslevhuus*.

Certain passages in *Der Schimmelreiter* may be cited as brilliant examples of virtually musical composition. Out of the huddled mass of men on the storm-swept dike, one shrill cry of mortal fear pierces the din of storm and sea; then one silent pointing figure, like a sign-post, compels all heads to turn; then Hauke's horrified cry is heard: "Herr Gott! Ein Bruch, ein Bruch!"; then an antiphonal accusing voice from the crowd: "Euere Schuld, Deichgraf, euere Schuld! Nehmt's mit vor Gottes Thron!" And this is re-echoed a moment later by Hauke: "Herr Gott, ja, ich bekenn es!" (372f.). The use of voices and repetitions here has a distinctly musical character.

Virtuosity in the use of sounds is abundantly apparent in this prose. We are made to feel the horror that still broods over the desolate strand where the hideous corpses lay, and the loneliness into which the boy ventures: a spell is woven with vowel and consonant sounds and rhythms and words of "mood-value:" "Er lief weiter und weiter, bis er einsam in der Öde stand, wo nur die Winde über den Deich wehten, wo nichts war als die klagenden Stimmen der grossen Vögel, die rasch vorüberschossen; zu seiner Linken die leere weite Marsch, zur andern Seite der unabsehbare Strand mit seiner jetzt vom Eise schimmernden Fläche der Watten; es war, als liege die ganze Welt in weissem Tod" (262).

One notes the "spell-weaving" effect of repetitions and low vowels in such a passage as this: "Über das ganze Watt spann sich ein Netz von Dampf und Nebel, das sich seltsam mit der Dämmerung des Abends mischte. Hauke sah mit starren Augen darauf hin; denn in dem Nebel schritten dunkle Gestalten auf und ab, sie schienen ihm so gross wie Menschen. Würdevoll, aber mit seltsamen, erschreckenden Gebärden; mit langen Nasen und Hälsen sah er sie fern an den rauchenden Spalten auf und ab spazieren; plötzlich begannen sie wie Narren unheimlich auf und ab zu springen, die grossen über die kleinen und die kleinen gegen die grossen; dann breiteten sie sich aus und verloren alle Form" (263).

Or, again, alliterating consonants, particularly sibilants, heighten the vague mood of moonlight and mystery: "Der Mond stand hoch am Himmel und beschien das weite Wattenmeer, das eben in der steigenden Flut seine Wasser über die glitzernden Schlickflächen zu spülen begann. Nur das leise Geräusch des Wassers, keine Tierstimme war in der ungeheuren Weite hier zu hören; auch in der Marsch, hinter dem Deiche, war es leer. Nichts regte sich; nur was sie für ein Pferd, einen Schimmel, hielten, schien dort auf Jevershallig noch beweglich. 'Es wird heller,' unterbrach der Knecht die Stille; 'ich sehe deutlich die weissen Schafgerippe schimmern'" (317).

Emphatic repetitions, alliterations, and sound-words reproduce the fearful music of the storm: "Eine furchtbare Böe kam brüllend vom Meer herüber, und ihr entgegen stürmten Ross und Reiter den schmalen Akt zum Deich hinan. Als sie oben waren, stoppte Hauke mit Gewalt sein Pferd. Aber wo war das Meer? Wo Jeverssand? Wo blieb das Ufer drüben?—Nur Berge von Wasser sah er vor sich, die dräuend gegen den nächtlichen Himmel stiegen, die in der furchtbaren Dämmerung sich über einander zu türmen suchten und über einander gegen das feste Land schlugen. Mit weissen Kronen kamen sie daher, heulend, als sei in ihnen der Schrei alles furchtbaren Raubgetiers der Wildnis" (369f.).[14]

The inherent musicality of Storm's work is evidenced also by his reiteration of characterizing details in the manner of a leitmotif, perhaps the most striking feature of his style in *Der Schimmelreiter*. Thus the withered crone Trin Jans is first shown cursing Hauke with her uplifted "mageren Arm" (266); then again, beating the air "mit ihren alten Händen" (287); she wipes her eyes "mit ihrer von Gicht gekrümmten Hand" (268), she points "mit ihrem verkrümmten Finger" (348), and finally she stretches out "ihre knöchernen Arme" and expires (363). Her son's motif comes in from time to time as that of the drowned sailor (264, 266, 268, 348, 363) and is connected with the motifs of the dangerous northwest wind and the sinister sea; he exemplifies the irony of human fate, surviving far voyages to drown at last at his mother's door.

Our attention is early called to Hauke's "aufgeschossene Gestalt" (261), and thereafter he re-enters as "ein langer, hagerer Bursche" (264), "der lang aufgeschossene Hauke" (271), "die hagere Gestalt ... das lange Friesengesicht" (288), "die lange Friesengestalt mit ... der hageren Nase und den zwei Schädelwölbungen darüber" (304)—a salient representative of his race. While yet alive, he assumes the lineaments of legend: "wie aus dem hageren Gesicht die Augen starrten, wie sein Mantel flog und wie der Schimmel sprühte!" (334; cf. 254). Again we see "seine hagere Gestalt auf dem feurigen Schimmel" (341); "aus dem hageren Gesicht des Deichgrafen sprühte der Zorn" (342). This attribute of "Hagerkeit" he shares with his father (274), his wife (270, 271), and his horse (254). His spurring of his horse is a very frequent motif, expressive of his energy and impatience, as his flashing eyes indicate his mental intensity.

Elke is introduced as a slim girl with brunette complexion and dark eyebrows that meet over her nose: "das ranke ... Mädchen mit dem bräunlichen schmalen Antlitz und den dunklen Brauen, die über ... der schmalen Nase in einander liefen" (271). In these terms we hear of her again: "das bräunliche Mädchen" (271), "das schmale Gesicht des Mädchens" (276), "die dunklen Brauen des Mädchens" (281), "das Mädchen mit den Rätselbrauen" (286), "die dunklen Brauen" knit in anger (289) or smoothed as she looks up at Hauke "mit ihrem schmalen Antlitz" (291). Her hand, likewise, is important, as it often is with Storm's women—the modern cult of the hand begins with him—; we hear of her "kleine Hand" (288, 289) and her "schmale Hand" (300, 330). One of her favorite gestures is the stroking of her hand over Hauke's cheek or brow (313, 330, 355).[15] Throughout her life and her husband's runs the motif of unremitting "Arbeit" (e.g., 269, 299, 307, 313, 314, 322, 331, 338). These two, like the father in *Hans und Heinz Kirch*, exemplify the tragedy of devotion to duty and work.

Elke's dominant trait is faithfulness, and from this point of view the story might be called a glorification of "Gattentreue." "Bleib mir treu, Elke, bleib mir treu!" cries Hauke, despairing of the good-will of others, and she answers "Dir treu? Wem sollt ich denn anders treu sein?" And then, grasping his deeper meaning, she adds, "Ja, wir sind uns treu; nicht nur, weil wir uns brauchen" (338). Ironically, it is her chief virtue that brings on her doom: her love and anxiety for Hauke drive her forth from her safe retreat into death; "O Elke, o getreue Elke!" is her epitaph from the lips of her husband (374). Storm's lifelong theme of love may be said to reach its maturest expression in the union of these two people.

Intellectual superiority sets them apart from their fellowmen and draws them together. "Sie waren beide geborene Rechner," and therefore instinctively comrades, suggests the Schoolmaster (275); and this motif of the "gute Rechner" runs all through the story. The old dikegrave is stupid, Hauke grants, "aber seine Tochter Elke, die kann rechnen!" (270); "die rechnet mich dreimal um und um," says her father (274); "ich kann ja nur rechnen," she herself says modestly (281). Hauke calculates that he can "take a hand in the reckoning" of that household (270). He is known as a youth who prefers the "Rechentafel" to brandy (273), and his "Rechengabe" is the decisive factor in his hiring and advancement (274f., 293). His chief adversary hates him for a "Schreiberknecht" (276, 339), and later, in office, he is opposed by the dullards as "der kluge Deichgraf, der immer grübeln geht" (308). "Vertrauet unserm Deichgrafen," Ole Peters remarks with bitter sarcasm, "der versteht zu rechnen!" (331). Herein, too, Hauke, "der kluge Friese" (300), is the conspicuous example of his race, for it is well known "die Friesen rechnen gut" (257). It is typical of Hauke to calculate (310), to keep a level head (293, 311), to think things out clearly (314). Even his peculiar type of Christianity he had "zurecht gerechnet" for himself (335). When he allows his mind to be muddled (358), he becomes untrue to Elke as well as to himself, and his tragedy is sealed when, with guilty fear of her bright intelligence, he refuses for the first time to confide in her (360). It is in keeping with the irony pervading the story that this man, the very exemplar of human reason in combat with the irrational, should become, even in his lifetime, a figure of diabolical myth, and that the only child of these two supremely intelligent people should be an imbecile.

A theme that runs through *Der Schimmelreiter* as well as other tales of Storm's is one that might be called "the theme of the hostile public." The power of prejudice, malicious gossip, stupidity, and superstition to wreck the lives of good, especially intellectually distinguished individuals, appears to have impressed Storm deeply. Already as a boy set apart from his contemporaries (261), and destined as a man to live and fight alone, Hauke is worn down by incessant opposition. When he is no longer opposed, it is a sign that he is on the wrong road (361). Before he undertakes his great project, Elke tells him that the public will be hostile and ungrateful (312), and thus it turns out (334, 376). Against him is arrayed the stolid anonymity of the mass that will not brook individuality, that wants no one singled out for blame (343) or even for praise (333f.). An unsocial hatred is engendered in Hauke; he becomes subject to a sort of hallucination of hostile faces: "Eine Reihe von Gesichtern ging vor seinem innern Blick vorüber, und sie sahen ihn alle mit bösen Augen an" (299). Again, when he feels the sting of slander, "ging vor seinem innern Auge die Reihe übelwollender Gesichter vorüber" (308). He and Elke see these hateful people snatching away their child, if they had one, for a living sacrifice (312). Hauke, saving a dog from this fate, again finds himself encircled by the hostile faces (343). At the last the greater adversary, the ocean, engulfs him and his wife and child, and never yields up their bodies, so that they are forever removed from hostile humanity (376).

The nature-background of the story is dominated by the motif of the sea: it is always visible or audible, and its breath is felt throughout these pages. Everything is mysteriously related to the sea. When we first glimpse Elke, she is gazing out to sea (271). When Hauke first mounts his Schimmel, it makes instantly for the dike, and tosses its head in greeting toward the sea (324), as if to confirm the popular belief in its resurrection from the bleached bones on the flooded island. The sea is a part of that vast realm of peril that surrounds man's little world; it is the fringe of that "Nichts" into which we go without return or reunion. "Wasser, das Wasser!" wails Elke, as in her delirium she sees Hauke carried out to sea and lost (335); and, as if the sea-terror could inherit, her child echoes the cry on its first sight of the ocean: "Wasser, Vater, das Wasser!" (351). The sea's silvery surface, lifted by a mirage, looks in upon the death of old Trin, bringing with it the motif of the ghostly island and the motif of the drowned sailor (362).

The ocean does not figure in *Der Schimmelreiter* as a habitable domain, as a path of commerce or a source of livelihood. Only once do we hear of fishing, and then it results in the death of the fisherman (266). No one ventures out on the water for pleasure. There is here none of the Romantic water-magic of *Eine Halligfahrt*, none of the salty pagan zest of *Psyche*. Casting up its dead or keeping them, the sea remains an alien and baleful thing. In this view, Storm's last Novelle echoes the first in which the ocean figures, *Auf dem Staatshof*, thirty years earlier.

With artistic symmetry, the immense expanse of water is paired with the broad reaches of land inside the dike: "die weite Marsch" and "das weite Wattenmeer" are recurrent phrases. At the very beginning, the Traveller finds himself between these twin desolations. The "weite Öde" of shore and sea becomes young Hauke's favorite resort (261, 264). Often no sound but the lapping of the tide is heard in that limitless solitude (317). Repetition conveys a sense of its vastness: "die leere, weite Marsch" (262), "die weite Gegend" (289), "die weite Weidefläche" (285), "die breite Landfläche" (310), "die ungeheure Weite" (317), "die weite Landschaft" (346). Silence weighs upon it; in the cold night the stars glitter "über der schweigenden Marsch" (292); darkness and stillness descend "über die ungeheure Ebene" (294); it lies "in lautlosem Schweigen" (320), or its "weite Stille" is broken by isolated lowings (339). We see "die weite Marsch" unveiled from white morning mists (344), or wrapped in the shadows of an ominous evening (368), or with its "unermessliche weissbereifte Weidefläche" spread under a winter moon (284). With the same impressive iteration we are shown "die unabsehbare, eisbedeckte Fläche der Watten" (262), "das weite Wattenmeer" (317), "die Watten breit, fast unabsehbar" (355), "die unabsehbaren Watten" (360).

With great artistry Storm weaves into his composition the motifs of sunlight and moonlight,[16] of scudding clouds and trailing mists. The wind blows in infinite modulations, a continuous obbligato to the action. Its most dangerous manifestation is the "Nordwest," which brings storm and disaster. Storm has various recurrent devices for conveying to the reader a feeling of the force of the wind: it tugs at the rider on the dike, threatening to blow him off his horse; it rattles windows and shutters; it flutters dresses and mantles; it tosses branches and hair. One feels its constant pressure on the consciousness and the lives of these seacoast-dwellers.

Linked with the wind-theme is that of the gulls. Storm-tossed and cackling, almost grazing the lone wayfarer with their long wings, they add to the wild mood of the opening scene (253). Again, wheeling in graceful flight, they connote the peace that follows storm (344), or conspire with Nature's deceptive aspect of benignity (360). They companion the lonely boy on the dike (259, 261), they witness his play and his work (289, 334), they scream mockingly as he crushes a half-tamed brother of their flock (368), and their skirling cries still attend his wraith on nights of storm (297).[17]

The motif of lights is used, naturally enough, to signify the security of home and social living. With a sense of relief the Traveller greets the lights of village and inn (254). Two candles always burning on the table of the dikegrave's house attest its importance and prosperity (276, 296); later, the storm invades it and symbolically extinguishes one of the candles (366). Festive lights blaze at the dance (290). In the moonless dark, the despairing Hauke sees a lone light beaming toward him, like a greeting from wife and child (373); and other lights from the upland denote the safety of the villagers (373). Again his eye meets the comforting gleam (374).[18] But his loved ones drown, and though the light still shines from his house, the soul has gone out of it (375). He too chooses death, and thereafter, as the final touch in his story, we see the distant light casting its trembling reflexes over the churning waves (375).

Another symbol of stability is the gigantic ash-tree, a poetic scion of the "Weltesche," that stands before the Deichgrafenhaus as the token of its predominance. It is the tallest tree in the village, and from it one can survey the whole bay (271, 348). It is the only survivor of three of its kind, signifying three generations of the "ruling family." It stands for tradition: its leaves, rustling in the incessant wind of this coast, seem to tell of bygone times (271). Under it Hauke and Elke stand as they speak of the decline of their fathers (293).[19] A rising wind, like an omen of trouble, shakes its branches (294). Its murmuring accompanies the fortunes of the house (307). When Hauke brings home the portentous Schimmel, he halts under the ash-tree (320). It becomes a seat of honor for little Wienke (340). In the final storm, it suffers a mortal strain, like the family it symbolizes: "die alte Esche knarrte, als ob sie aus einander stürzen solle" (367). In a concluding picture, we see its boughs wildly whipping the air, while Elke clings to its trunk and looks off after Hauke on his last ride seaward—an eloquent allegory of forlornness and approaching doom (367).[20]

All Storm's writings, including his letters, bear witness to his high regard for the eye as the mirror of the soul. In *Der Schimmelreiter*, however, he has given this motif unique importance as a means of characterization and communication. Disregarding situations where mention of eyes is inevitable in ordinary usage, one can count scores of instances of this emphatic employment. The keen little Schoolmaster is signalized at once by his bright eyes (256), and his "kleine, kluge Augen" (264), "seine klugen Augen" (298), "seine feinen Augen" (314) recur as his most significant attribute. Old Trin is distinguished by her "funkelnden Augen" (267, 268), the hostile public by its "böse Augen" (299), and Hauke's eyes in return "Sahen grimmig zur Seite" (308) in the manner of the sinister Gaspard of *Haderslevhuus*. The nurse regards Hauke "mit entsetzten Augen" (336); the stable-boy's terror is written in his "erschrokkenen Augen" (321); on Elke's recovery the doctor's "alte Augen lachten" (337); the shrewd Pastorin watches Elke's eyes intently (301); old Volkert's eyes "quellen wie Glaskugeln" in unwonted mental effort (270). The black eyes of the gulls (259) and the green eyes of the big cat (268) are called to our notice.

The eyes of the Schimmel when first seen are dull and sunken and "blöde" (320, 322); they plead with Hauke for pity (323). Restored to good condition, its eyes prove to be brown and lustrous (324, 339) and of expressive beauty (324, 334). The eyes of little Wienke, on the other hand, remain lustreless and "stumpf" (340, 355), in sad contrast to the bright-eyed child of Elke's charwoman (340); they are pale (351, 363) and apathetic (348) and too quiet (353), though on occasion they can express gratitude for a caress (349) or bewilderment and fear (351, 356).

The taciturn boy Hauke uses a glance in place of words (258, 260); the peculiar expression of his eyes stays Ole Peters's bullying (275). His acute intelligence shows in his "scharfe," "rasche," "durchdringende Augen" (279, 371, 336); they reveal prodigious brainwork going on behind them (309). His eyes can be happy (296), or angry (371), or they can have the far-away look of the visionary (309). Most often they are spoken of as "fest" (272, 288, 346) and "klug" and "grau" (288, 291, 296, 304); and finally we see them aglow with the light of his last battle (366).

When Hauke first sees Elke, he is impressed by her "grosse Augen" (271). As his eyes are most often alluded to as shrewd and grey, so hers are regularly described as shrewd and dark (273, 278, 282, 296, 305, 322, 337, 367). They express a variety of emotions: they can be defiant (271), angry (286), serious (307, 312), wild with fever (336), radiant with joy (337), wide with astonishment (338), roguish (312), laughing (339, 340); a source of comfort and courage to her husband, and again wells of unfathomable grief (352).

At times these two communicate only with their eyes (276). Hauke cannot declare his love with words; his eyes must speak for him (291); she lowers hers lest they betray her; and then "ein Blick, mit der stillen Kraft ihres Wesens, traf in die seinen" and gives her answer (292). Often her emotion at his safe return from danger is shown only through "ein leuchtender Blitz aus ihren sonst so stillen Augen" (313f.). The deep understanding of these almost perfectly mated souls speaks in their eyes, and it is thus they take their last farewell: "Sie erhob langsam ihre dunklen Augen zu ihm, und ein paar Sekunden lang sahen sie sich an; doch war's wie eine Ewigkeit" (367).

This characteristic motif of the "eloquent eye," observable in other stories of Storm's, is most fully developed in *Der Schimmelreiter*, and in this respect, also, his last work may be said to mark the culmination of his narrative art. The use of such motifs, moreover, as we have seen in other instances, is eminently characteristic of the high compositional art of the Novelle as such. Whether it borrows from the plastic objectivity of drama or the musical reminiscences of opera, or the vivid scenic force of both, or, again, from the pregnant symbolism of lyrical utterance—in every case the Novelle employs, as it were instinctively, devices that make for concentration and enhancement.

CHAPTER TEN
HAUPTMANN, *BAHNWÄRTER THIEL* (1887)

With Gerhart Hauptmann's Novelle *Bahnwärter Thiel* we stand at the threshold of a new age in German literature, the period of "Naturalismus" that was to succeed "Poetischer Realismus." The little story was written and published in 1887, the year in which Berlin saw the performances of the visiting *Théâtre libre* that were to lead two years later to the establishment of the "Freie Bühne" and the debut of its chief talent, the young dramatist Hauptmann who quickly came to be regarded as the leader of the new literary revolt.

Bahnwärter Thiel, however, precedes that year of committal. It is a Janus-faced work, with traits both of the era which is coming to a close and of the era which is about to open. This makes it especially meaningful and appropriate as a termination for our present series of studies. In Hauptmann's life, too, it comes out of the middle of a critical period of transition, the Erkner years (1885-1888) which Hauptmann himself in his *Lebenserinnerungen* entitles "Lebenswende." It is Hauptmann's first narrative work, little regarded then or since because of the more sensational plays and longer stories that followed it; and yet it is a real masterpiece, and we can see in it already characteristic features of Hauptmann's style and of his *Weltanschauung.*

The young author of twenty-four, modestly conscious of being a beginner, entitled his tale a "novellistische Studie," not a Novelle outright. But it is a genuine Novelle nevertheless, fulfilling an unusual number of the familiar requirements of this "Gattung." It is brief (only thirty-seven pages in the standard edition) and limited in time, place, and action. It deals with only two, or at most three, adult persons. Strictly speaking, there is no evolution of character, as in the novel, but the revelation of a hitherto submerged side of character under the impact of crisis. There is a striking central event (the death of little Tobias), "eine sich ereignete, unerhörte Begebenheit" in Goethe's terms, and we are shown its effect on an already matured or "fertig" hero. There is a distinct "Wendepunkt" in the middle of the story: Thiel's first vision of his dead wife, which is the first mental objectivation of the feeling of guilt and unfaithfulness that eventuates in murder. An "Idee" summarizing the action could readily be compressed into a brief and arresting statement. There are a number of impressive "Leitmotive," and one of these, Tobias's pathetic little brown cap, could qualify as a "Falke" in Heyse's sense. Certainly the story has the "scharfe Silhouette" stipulated by Heyse: its world, centered around a remote stretch of railroad-track and isolated by silent forest and solitude that encourage inward life, has a vivid and unique individuality. In this case, there is no "Rahmen" or frame; the author is "omniscient," but his presence is never suggested; there is complete objectivity of report.

The nature of the Novelle, as we have observed, favors dramatic procedures, and in *Bahnwärter Thiel* also one can pick out dramatic passages, such as the scene of the accident, where the author resorts to the lively present tense, some dialogue, and virtual "stage-directions."[1] In the weirdly "acted" brief scene on the tracks (41f.) we see only Thiel excitedly speaking and gesticulating, but are made vividly aware of the unseen "other one;" here, as in Kleist's *Bettelweib von Locarno*, one feels the hand of the dramatist. We are "present" at this scene, whereas Thiel's earlier vision came in a dream and was merely reported to us.

Yet, despite these occasional pseudo-dramatic interludes, the technique in *Bahnwärter Thiel* is decidedly epic. There is very little dialogue. Speech is often quoted, as in Kleist's Novellen, indirectly, in the subjunctive; the only direct speech of any considerable length is Lene's tirade against little Tobias (21f.). There is no "build-up" to scenes, but straightforward narrative procedure. Yet the story has a strongly propulsive action and intensification; it rises steadily, with "rest-periods" of description, to a climactic, explosive ending. The descriptive passages, for their part, are never allowed to become static or ends in themselves, but are integrated with the action, physical and above all psychological.

Throughout, Hauptmann maintains an even, epic tenor of factual report. His sentences are never very long, and are admirably clear and simple in structure. In climaxes of great emotional tension, like the account of the fatal accident, the sentences become even shorter, some consisting of three words, two words, even one word:

>Er ist es.
>Thiel spricht nicht. Sein Gesicht nimmt eine schmutzige Blässe an. Er lächelt wie abwesend; endlich beugt

er sich; er fühlt die schlaffen, toten Gliedmassen schwer in seinen Armen; die rote Fahne wickelt sich darum. Er geht.
Wohin?
"Zum Bahnarzt, zum Bahnarzt," tönt es durcheinander.
"Wir nehmen ihn gleich mit," ruft der Packmeister und macht in seinem Wagen aus Dienströcken und Büchern ein Lager zurecht. "Nun also?"
Thiel macht keine Anstalten, den Verunglückten loszulassen. Man drängt in ihn. Vergebens. Der Packmeister lässt eine Bahre aus dem Packwagen reichen und beordert einen Mann, dem Vater beizustehen.
Die Zeit ist kostbar. Die Pfeife des Zugführers trillert. Münzen regnen aus den Fenstern.
Lene gebärdet sich wie wahnsinnig (38).

An impressive device of style, but one that is not overused (as it may be said to have been, for example, in Brentano's Novelle), is that of the leitmotif. The great unbroken expanses of forest are thought of as a sea, and we hear of "ein schwarzgrünes, wellenwerfendes Meer" (20), "das schwarzgrüne Wipfelmeer" (26), or the forest surging "wie Meeresbrandung" in the tempest (28). The "Meldeglocke" that rings in the booth to announce the oncoming trains is heard repeatedly, and Thiel responds unfailingly; thus the motif contributes both to *milieu* and to characterization. The brown "Plüschmützchen" is emblematic of little Tobias and the mood of his one pathetic holiday; it becomes the fetish of the insane father, and the last, telling picture focuses our attention on this eloquent object.

Allied to the leitmotif is another device that might perhaps better be called correspondence or echoing, since it involves only two correspondent points and not a series. Thus we hear, early in the story, of a "Rehbock" that was run down by a train one winter night (15f.). Near the end of the story (44f.) a fine buck is shown leading his herd safely over the tracks that have just proved fatal to Tobias. Is an irony intended in the fact that Nature's creature heeds the danger-signal to which the child of Man did not respond?[2] Or are the two occurrences meant to show the same impersonal, now destructive now benevolent, operation of natural law that *Abdias* demonstrated? In any case, the "recall" has an artistic effect. The motif of "schwarzes Blut" on Tobias's lips (38) sets a pattern for Thiel's fell intent against Lene (41). In similar sinister fashion, the association "Eichhörnchen—der liebe Gott" (35), when it recurs, sets off a murderous reaction (43). On the way to the field, Thiel pushes the baby-carriage with an effort through the sand (33); on the sad return trip, it is Lene who does the same (45); the tragic events that the day has brought are thus tacitly signalized.

There is a striking use of sound-effects in the story; indeed, one would suspect it to be the work of a musically rather than sculpturally gifted writer. The account of the approach of the Breslau-Berlin express might be called a "Virtuosenstück" in this regard:

> Durch die Geleise ging ein Vibrieren und Summen, ein rhythmisches Geklirr, ein dumpfes Getöse, das, lauter und lauter werdend, zuletzt den Hufschlägen eines heranbrausenden Reitergeschwaders nicht unähnlich war.
>
> Ein Keuchen und Brausen schwoll stossweise ferner durch die Luft. Dann plötzlich zerriss die Stille. Ein rasendes Tosen und Toben erfüllte den Raum, die Geleise bogen sich, die Erde zitterte—ein starker Luftdruck—eine Wolke von Staub, Dampf und Qualm, und das schwarze, schnaubende Ungetüm war vorüber. So wie sie anwuchsen, starben nach und nach die Geräusche (26).

Or, again, the crescendo of the thunder, as it first awakens on the distant horizon and then draws nearer and increases, until its mighty voice fills the whole air and shakes the solid earth (29). There are passages of cacophony such as the braking and stopping of the work-train (44). On the other hand there are instances of verbal music that bear comparison with Storm's, especially in the alliteration on both vowels and consonants:

> Die Kiefern bogen sich und rieben unheimlich knarrend und quietschend ihre Zweige aneinander. Einen Augenblick wurde der Mond sichtbar, wie er gleich einer blassgoldenen Schale zwischen den Wolken lag. In seinem Lichte sah man das Wühlen des Windes in den schwarzen Kronen der Kiefern. Die Blattgehänge der Birken am Bahndamm wehten und flatterten wie gespenstige Rossschweife. Darunter lagen die Linien der

Geleise, welche, von Nässe glänzend, das blasse Mondlicht in einzelnen Flecken aufsogen (29).

One could call *Bahnwärter Thiel* the earliest Novelle of Naturalism, and adduce enough evidence from it to justify this classification. After these naturalistic elements had been extracted, however, there would be enough others left to make out a case for *Bahnwärter Thiel* as a work of Poetic Realism. The *milieu* of much of the story is typical of Naturalism. The picture of the "Arbeiterkolonie" on the Spree outside Berlin,[3] and the "close-up" of Thiel's own dwelling and his home life with its daily routine and its marital "scenes," all presented in factual, unvarnished detail, belongs to Naturalism, which preferred to emphasize the sordid and depressing aspects of lower-class life. Nothing of beauty or poetry is shown here, but a dull, unrelieved vulgarity. The hopelessness of Thiel's situation, the lack of "horizon" or mental resource, are characteristic of the atmosphere of Naturalism.

Furthermore, it may be thought indicative of the naturalistic trend in the story that, though the essential action is inward, it is set in a social matrix. We are constantly kept aware of a public, though this is, characteristically, anonymous and not even represented by typical individuals. There is a running commentary of public opinion, which is for the most part treated with light satire, as being based on very superficial evidence. "Wie die Leute meinten," Thiel's first wife was not at all suitable for him—because of the difference in their physiques (11). "Wie die Leute versicherten," Thiel was unaffected by her death —for were not his brass buttons as brightly polished, his red hair as sleeked, as ever (11)? "Die Leute," again on surface evidence, approve of his second choice: Lene is thought an ideal partner for him (12). Later, to be sure, the opinion of the neighborhood becomes more critical of her. "Die Leute" also censure Thiel for devoting so much time to the dirty brats (Rotznasen) of the settlement (19). After the accident to Tobias, Lene, whose callousness and hostility to the boy really caused his death, gets credit with the train passengers as "die arme, arme Mutter" (38), simply because of the way she "takes on," while the dazed and silent Thiel is comparatively unnoticed. At the end, the neighbors ("man") discover the frightful denouement, and its effect on them is reflected to us.

All the people in the story belong to the working class. We

are not yet dealing with city "Proletariat," however; Thiel's neighbors are not factory workers, but fishermen and outdoor laborers. The author, to be sure, speaks of the collection of twenty houses (with a store in one room of one of them) as a "Dorf," but it is little better than a suburban slum, and we are conscious of the nearby metropolis, to which Thiel is finally transported. Nature itself is effete here, without the vigor of the true countryside; we see the river in the background, flowing sluggishly, black and glassy between scantily-leaved poplars (19). We get a glimpse of the village street, with the storekeeper's mangy dog lying in the middle of it and a crow flapping overhead with raucous cries (21). We see Thiel's little cottage, with its low cracked ceilings and narrow steep stairs. As we approach it, we are likely to hear the strident voice of Lene, the former "Kuhmagd," raised in vituperation. Coarse, burly, sensual, brutally passionate, domineering, and quarrelsome, she is a drastic contrast to Thiel's first wife, Minna, the quiet, frail, and spiritual.[4]

Lene climaxes a flood of vilification of her little stepson by spitting at the child (22). Her excitement in this scene brings out her voluptuous physical charms before her husband's spellbound eyes: we see "das Tier" in its full flush. We see her again spading the potato-patch, stopping only to nurse her child, with panting, sweat-dripping breast (34). Our last view is of her lying in her blood, her skull crushed, her face unrecognizable, butchered with the kitchen hatchet (47).

Of equally unsparing naturalism is the portrait of little Tobias, with his overgrown head and spindling limbs, his yellowish-red hair and chalky complexion and bloodless lips; in his bed, pestered with flies, or eating plaster out of cracks in the wall—a pitiable and at the same time repellent figure of an undernourished, abused, and almost cretinous child. Hauptmann does not spare us the details of the fatal accident: Tobias being tossed about between the wheels, the train grinding to a stop, the commotion and outcry, and finally a close-up picture of the horribly mangled and twisted little body on the stretcher.

This is "naturalistic" writing, no doubt of it. But Hauptmann was not only a Naturalist, and it may be questioned whether he was ever a very "consistent" one. "Konsequenter Naturalismus" calls for an undiscriminating and total "Wiedergabe" or reproduction of life, with no intrusion of the author's subjectivity and no factor of artistic selection. Naturalism of this "purity" is of course only theoretically possible. No real poet has ever been able to eliminate his artistic individuality from his work, and Naturalism itself could not dispense with selection; only it was resolved to select the sordid in human life, to the denial of every poetic element—and thus misrepresented the world quite as badly as did the most supernal idealists.

But there was a Poetic Realist left in Hauptmann. Indeed, one might say that in all periods of his life he betrays, like Goethe, a latent Romanticism. And one can prove both assertions by reference to *Bahnwärter Thiel*. The action in this story is chiefly an inner, psychological action, as it is in Ludwig's *Zwischen Himmel und Erde*; its "reality" is essentially that of the mind. It is significant that the most violent happening, the brutal murder of Lene and her infant, after being fully motivated psychologically, is not offered to our view as an act, but only in its results. The starkly sensual love between Thiel and Lene is strongly suggested, but not depicted, as outright Naturalism would have demanded. And the diction of all the persons in the story is kept above the low level of their actual speech.

The things of Nature, too, are not seen materially, but as they affect the mind. The forest is not a source of livelihood or timber; it has no social or economic value at all, but a personal, poetic, religious one. When the din of Man and his machine has died away, Nature resumes its ancient solitary reign: "das alte heil'ge Schweigen schlug über dem Waldwinkel zusammen" (26)—this is the language of Romanticism.

And Man's machine itself, the train, is to some extent poeticized and given symbolical value. The railroads when they first appeared seemed to late-Romanticists like Justinus Kerner an abomination, ringing the knell of all poetry in life. Here, a half-century later, they have become productive of poetic "Stimmung" and wonder. Details of this railroad world are sharply seen and recorded, even to the number of bolts in a section of rail (36) or the items of equipment in the crossing-tender's shed. The phenomena of perspective, as they appear in the patterns of the right-of-way or in the oncoming and receding of a fast train; the "lag" in the sound that follows the white steam-puff of the whistle; the various noises of wheels and brakes and crunching gravel—all these are specific and exact.

And yet the account is shot through with imaginative comparisons: the floods of fog recoil from the embankment like a surf; the rails are strands in a vast iron net or, again, fiery snakes in the sunset red; the telegraph poles give forth mysterious chords, and the wires are like the web of some gigantic spider. The "panting" of a work-train locomotive slowing to a stop is like the heavy, agonized breathing of a sick giant. One can think, for contrast, of what a later realist would have made of "the tracks" as a scene of squalor and crime. But Hauptmann frames his stage with "Wald"—the very word, with all its connotations, cannot be fully rendered by an English one—and trains and tracks and telegraph poles are still things of much mystery and poetry, set in Nature.

The importance attached in this story to "Beruf" or calling is another trait characteristic of Poetic Realism. It appears in the very name of the hero; it is a part of his personality. More important than the external trappings of uniform and cartridge-pouch and red flag are the qualities of character that fit Thiel for his work: his neatness, orderliness, and punctuality, symbolized by his old-fashioned but accurate watch and by the signal-bell to which he responds even under the most trying circumstances. Thiel does not yet typify the modern employee nor a class-conscious proletariat nor organized labor. He has still something of the loyal retainer of an earlier age. He belongs with Ludwig's forester Ulrich or slater Apollonius, men whose heart is in their work, and to whom "Beruf" has much of its old, full meaning of work to which one is called.

Thiel lives in two separate worlds. His actual "Wohnung" in the river "colony" is for sleeping and eating and the gratification of sex; but his spiritual home is the little booth on the lonely stretch of track, an island of inwardness and "Erhebung" set in a vast dark-green sea of forest. Nowhere else is Hauptmann's heritage from Romanticism so evident as in his use of the "Wald," even to the old magical word "Waldeinsamkeit" (24), which takes us straight back to Tieck and Eichendorff.

Throughout the story, the Nature-background is kept in view. There is a rich variety of "Naturstimmungen," and these moods of Nature are related to the states of mind of the persons, especially the hero. This linking of man with his natural out-of-doors setting is a persistence of Poetic Realism, quite different from the metropolitan *milieu* of which Naturalism became so fond. With its glorious sunrises and sunsets, Nature draws

Thiel's soul out into infinite spaces; and then again with its winter storms it shuts him in to plumb the equally infinite depths of his soul and rise to mystic heights of ecstasy and vision. A stormy night with lightning and wind-tossed trees forms a background and parallel to his inner upheaval. A radiant morning that follows, with floods of sunlight and the sleepy dripping of dew from the leaves, helps to assuage his sense of guilt and impending tragedy. After the frightful accident, Nature itself seems paralyzed with horror: "Es ist still ringsum geworden, totenstill; schwarz und heiss ruhen die Geleise auf dem blendenden Kies. Der Mittag hat die Winde erstickt, und regungslos wie aus Stein steht der Forst" (39).

For the desolate scene of the work-train returning with Tobias's body a fit stage-setting is briefly indicated: "Ein kaltes Zwielicht lag über der Gegend" (43). As the stretcher with the unconscious Thiel is carried through the woods, the reddish moon pales to a funeral lamp, giving the faces of the little company a cadaverous cast, and its pallid light is swallowed up in the dark basins of the clearings (45). Sometimes a nature-scene is interpolated as "relief" after a scene of violence. Thus, after Thiel's second vision of Minna, which ends with the compulsive idea of a savage murder, we read: "Ein sanfter Abendhauch strich leis und nachhaltig über den Forst, und rosaflammiges Wolkengelock hing über dem westlichen Himmel" (41f.). Or, just before the catastrophe, there is a delicate picture of springtime Nature that might have come out of the late-Romantic world of Storm's *Immensee:* "Stücke blauen Himmels schienen auf den Boden des Haines herabgesunken, so wunderbar dicht standen kleine, blaue Blüten darauf. Farbigen Wimpeln gleich flatterten und gaukelten die Schmetterlinge lautlos zwischen dem leuchtenden Weiss der Stämme, indes durch die zart grünen Blätterwolken der Birkenkronen ein sanftes Rieseln ging" (35).

To the field of modern realism, on the other hand, belong the many small details of everyday living that characterize the hero in his outward appearance and demeanor, and the psychological finesse with which his inner life is exposed. Thiel is an orderly and dutiful man, slow, given to routine and set habits—for years the various things he carries in his pockets have been laid out on his dresser in a fixed order, and go back in that order (20). He has an animal-like patience and a childlike good-nature, a big and muscular frame, and coarse-cut features that nevertheless reflect "soul." He is a person of "mystische Neigungen," which are fostered by the isolation of his place of work and the uneventful monotony of his outward existence. With this religious-mystical bent is linked a sensitive, if inarticulate, feeling for Nature and a musical sense: listening raptly to the mysterious harmonies that issue from the telegraph poles, he can fancy himself in church, or in Heaven (35).

Outer events appear to make little impression on Thiel; he seems to possess infinite inner compensations: "Die Aussenwelt schien ihm wenig anhaben zu können: es war, als trüge er etwas in sich, wodurch er alles Böse, was sie ihm antat, reichlich mit Gutem aufgewogen erhielt" (13). His powers of expression are extremely limited; things that do affect him, without outward sign, tend to "go down" and accumulate, and erupt later. He has something of the monumental simplicity and quietness of Brentano's Anna Margaret, and his slow, deep speech and "leiser, kühler Ton" (13) remind us of hers.

He reminds us also of another Common Man a half-century earlier, Büchner's Woyzeck, the most unheroic hero in the German drama up to his time. Both are simple, not to say simple-minded, faithful, "kinderlieb," inarticulate, concealing profound spiritual depths beneath a usually tranquil surface; easy-going, slow to suspicion and wrath, but finally capable of murderous violence against the women who have failed them. Lene also bears some resemblance to Woyzeck's Marie: a strapping, sensual woman, but one with a conscience and a capacity for acute contrition. Büchner, like Hauptmann, regards both these humble folk with deep compassion, though this feeling is not obtruded upon the narrative itself. It is interesting to recall that Hauptmann was one of the first "discoverers" of Büchner; just a few weeks after completing *Bahnwärter Thiel* he lectured on Büchner to the "Durch" literary club in Berlin, and he seems to have recognized Büchner as a literary forebear.[5]

Thiel exemplifies Faust's "zwei Seelen:" his consciousness is the battleground of man's spiritual and sensual natures, of sacred and profane love. He is a man placed in a sort of Grillparzerian triangle between two women of opposite types: one sickly, delicate, spiritual; the other robust, coarse, sensual. The two sides of his own nature correspond and respond to these two women: his pious, mystical, compassionate spirit to Minna; his brute strength and phlegma and primitive sensuality to Lene.

Minna dies in childbirth, leaving a continuation of her being in Tobias—for Thiel's relation to both is spiritual: they call forth his pity, devotion, and tenderness divorced from sex in the ordinary sense.

Thiel's other nature comes to the fore in his second marriage. He justifies this, to be sure, as a step for Tobias's benefit; this is the only reason he gives the pastor, and it seems sanctioned by Minna's dying injunction (12); but one suspects a certain amount of rationalization in all this. At any rate, Thiel falls under Lene's physical spell, at times so completely that he is utterly unnerved and callously ignores Tobias's sufferings. Troubled in conscience by this apostasy, he then "compensates" by increased attention to Tobias (which intensifies Lene's jealous dislike of the child to the pitch of hatred) and by converting his lonely gate-tender's booth into a sort of chapel consecrated to the memory of Minna. He divides his time conscientiously between the living and the dead, thus fulfilling his obligations to both women and both sides of his nature. He keeps his worlds completely separate, withholding from Lene any knowledge of the number and location of his booth and keeping her, on one pretext or another, from ever accompanying him thither (14).

This arrangement functions successfully for a long while, and Thiel achieves a satisfactory equilibrium; only at certain times, when he "comes out of" an especially deep communion with the dead in his lonely devotions, does he feel disgust at his "other" life (15). The crisis, however, comes one evening when it dawns upon his slow-working brain that, because of necessary arrangements about a potato-patch, Lene will be invading his sanctuary in the woods and destroying the precarious balance of his mental and moral existence. At this instant, a thick black curtain of self-deception seems to be rent asunder, and he sees clearly what he has committed as it were in a two years' trance (28). Under the pressure of agonized repentance, he experiences a dream-vision in which his suppressed guilt-feelings take terrifying shape, dream and reality merging so convincingly that he all but stops a speeding train to keep the apparition of Minna from being run over.

The necessities of "real" life, represented by the potatoes which are such an indispensable staple for the poor, soon compel an adjustment, to be sure, and Thiel seems to accept the inevitable with a good grace, even going so far as to let Lene eat lunch with him in the sacred booth (36). But the psychological trauma, inflicted by this desecration of the past and vitiation of his conditions for normal existence, has of course not been overcome on a deeper level, and when Lene's carelessness causes the death of Tobias, the "other" world rises in a second and more compelling vision (41f.), and at its behest Thiel wreaks vengeance with a savageness in which there is a large amount of "displaced" consciousness of his own guilt and perfidy.

The psychological sequences which Hauptmann presents are extraordinarily lifelike and convincing. As a result of a surprise return home (he had forgotten his lunch), Thiel witnesses Lene's mistreatment of Tobias, previous signs of which he had "suppressed;" but, succumbing to Lene's physical and sexual power, he retreats in silent defeat. He loses himself in his duties at the tracks, in the contemplation of a magnificent sunset and the passing of a train. This defense of distraction wears thin, however—the more so as Nature's silent solemnity has stirred the deeper religious levels of his mind—and suddenly the name "Minna" comes up from below, as yet without conscious connection, to his lips. He succeeds in dropping it, while he absently sips his coffee and reads a scrap of newspaper he had picked up along the track. He begins to feel restless, thinks it is due to the heat in the booth, takes off his coat and vest, then decides to "do something" to get relief. He starts to spade up the garden patch, and the physical exertion proves soothing. But then apropos of this patch the thought arises that now Lene can no longer be prevented from coming out here, his carefully built up compensation will be lost and his guilt-feeling revived. Now he hates the patch he was so joyful over. Hastily, as though he had been committing a sacrilege, he pulls the spade out of the ground and puts it away. He is ready to fight some "invader" of his sanctuary; his muscles tense, he utters a defiant laugh; startled by this sound, he loses his train of thought, but finds it again—or it finds him, one might say, and holds him. Now in a flash he must recognize the reality of the domestic situation he has so long evaded, above all the plight of Tobias, that legacy from his earlier, better life; and he is wrung with pity, remorse, and a deep sense of shame over his long bondage (23-28).

In Thiel, Hauptmann has given a tragically impressive picture of a man seeking (in this case with no great mental resources) to reconcile two conflicting sides of his given nature, the needs of the spirit and the needs of the flesh. The balance which Thiel has for a space achieved, in his simple way, seems so insecure that one feels, had the fatal mishap to Tobias not occurred, some other crisis would surely have developed. The frightful "justice" which he wreaks on Lene and her child does not avail to redress Thiel's balance, for it is either the result or the contributory cause of the insanity which marks the final collapse of all effort.

It may not be too fanciful to think of Thiel as a sort of "gesteigerter Spielmann." Both are fundamentally good men, dutiful, kind, patient, trusting, utterly simple, relatively defenseless, yet distinguished by an uncommonly strong and deep inner life. Both defend this inner life, to some extent successfully, against the assaults of the outside world. But with a difference: Thiel has gone all the way along the road on which Jakob has been able to reach a stopping-place. The delusion which helps to shield Jakob from reality has reached a pathological extreme in Thiel; "Wahn" has become "Wahnsinn." One might say that Thiel's insanity constitutes the soul's retreat, in the face of unbearable torment, into its innermost fastness, from which there is no return, but also no expulsion. Thiel demonstrates in ultimate and desperate terms the superior reality of ideas over the "facts" of life which we observed in gentler form in the case of the poor fiddler.

The problem that has not become tragic for Jakob because of his very "Untüchtigkeit" and "Selbstbescheidung," but that becomes destructive for Thiel, is the problem of sex. The obsession with this problem, and its disillusioned, not to say cynical treatment in *Bahnwärter Thiel,* is a mark of Naturalism and not of Poetic Realism. The "Problematik" of sex and marriage dominates the story, and in the last analysis it is sex as affliction, as a source of guilt and destruction, as it was to be represented, a few years after this, in the plays of Frank Wedekind.

Bahnwärter Thiel could be described as a kind of bitter allegory of Man persecuted by Woman. Thiel is tyrannized and enslaved no less by the continuing spiritual influence of his first wife than by the sensuality of the second. The spirit of the first mercilessly condemns his physical sexuality and mercilessly exacts murderous atonement: "black blood" for black blood. The body of the second seems to Thiel the very incarnation of sexual vitality, overpowering, enervating, inspiring in man a mixture of lust, fear, and resentment at subjugation. Between these two opposite types of woman, Thiel is ground to pieces as between an upper and a nether millstone. He achieves no full happiness with either, but only an overwhelming sense of guilt that drives him to murder and madness.

But to the two women, who destroy Thiel, sex likewise brings destruction. Each is cut off early by anguish and death as a result of her sexual nature, and the offspring of each perishes violently. All these sufferers are viewed by the young author with that compassion which was to become so characteristic of his subsequent work that Hauptmann has been called "der Dichter des Mitleids."

Compassion is a saving grace left to an age that has lost hope and belief in an ultimate meaning in events. For Storm, too, death meant final annihilation. Yet man's end was heroic, and his work survived him, and perpetuated his name. Here, nothing survives. There is no "Ausblick," no vista of a better future, no uplift or ennobling effect of tragedy, but only dumb brute suffering that terminates in dull, savage destruction. Here is a pessimism that outdoes even Grillparzer's. For the poor fiddler achieved a triumph of the spirit. He rose at the end to heroism, even in the conventional sense of the word, and he was assumed into Heaven: "der musiziert jetzt mit den lieben Engeln, die auch nicht viel besser sein können, als er."[6] Thiel's course is not upward, but downward, and a not merely material but mental deterioration. Jakob becomes a hero and a benefactor, Thiel a murderer and an inmate of an asylum for the criminally insane.

Der Schimmelreiter, for all its scepticism, still looks back to the great age of Idealism, with its faith in salient individuals and indestructible spiritual values; Hauke Haien is a great man with a mission, a brother to Kohlhaas. *Bahnwärter Thiel*, on the other hand, despite its residual Romanticism, looks out upon a new age of materialism, mass humanity, and social "conditions;" its hero is a "kleiner Mann" of no prominence or formidableness, whose end brings a shudder of pathos rather than the sharp, tonic thrill of high tragedy.

Though *Bahnwärter Thiel* was actually written shortly before *Der Schimmelreiter*, it impresses us as a decidedly more modern work. For one thing, it deals with a contemporary situation, *Der Schimmelreiter* with one of the eighteenth century. Storm's theme comes out of the mists of folk tradition; Hauptmann's might have come out of the morning's newspaper. *Der Schimmelreiter* concludes an epoch, *Bahnwärter Thiel* opens an epoch. The one is the last work of a man of seventy-one, the other the first work of a man of twenty-four;[7] the one ends, the other begins, a long literary lifetime. Brentano's *Kasperl und Annerl* appeared in the year of Storm's birth, *Bahnwärter Thiel* just seventy years later; within that span, one may say, lies the achievement of Poetic Realism.

But that age was now ended. *Der Schimmelreiter* is its last great monument in the Novelle, and Storm the last great literary exponent of its middle-class ideals: "Er steht an der Grenze und ist der Letzte der grossen deutschen bürgerlichen Literatur."[8] With the death of Gottfried Keller in 1890 the greatest of the Poetic Realists expires. Storm had died two years earlier; Meyer lived on eight years longer, but his productive powers were blighted after 1891. With the passing of these three supreme masters of its most successful embodiment—the Novelle—the great period of Poetic Realism comes to a close.

In other spheres, too, the year 1890 was a demarcation. In that year the self-confident young Emperor William II forced the retirement of the veteran statesman Bismarck, and launched Germany on the course that was to end in the disaster of two world wars. New forces were coming to the fore on the world's stage: imperialism, economic internationalism, socialism, big business, and a mechanization of life such as the writers of Poetic Realism could have had no conception of. In literature, a new era was inaugurated when in 1889 the "Neue freie Bühne" in Berlin presented Hauptmann's *Vor Sonnenaufgang* and Sudermann's *Ehre*. The "Bürgertum," which had formed the social basis and the center of interest for Poetic Realism, was supplanted by the urban proletariat, whose misery writers sought to reproduce with photographic exactitude, in place of the artistic reflection of reality which was the ideal of Keller's generation. If the Poetic Realists seemed old-fashioned to the adherents of Naturalism, these in turn have become old-fashioned in the perspective of a half-century that has seen Neo-Romanticism, Impressionism, Neo-Classicism, Expressionism, Neue Sachlichkeit, Magischer Realismus, and other "waves of the future" recede into eddies of the past.

The achievement of Poetic Realism, for a time obscured by its successors, shone forth again with heightened lustre—not because there was any specific virtue in its poetic theory, but because of the excellence of many of its poetic productions. Great literature is made by poets, not by theorists (a poet is, etymologically, a "maker;" a theorist, a "viewer"). We divide the history of literature, for convenience, into periods and movements, and we treat it, for convenience, in such divisions, as has been done in the present book. But such procedures are only scaffolding, or fencing-off, to enable us to get close to what counts most: the individual artistic creation.

The supreme test of all poetry ("Dichtung" in the broad German sense) is its power to body forth new beings and their environing worlds, persons who *were* not before the inspired vision saw them and fixed them with the inexplicable magic of words, making them more real than the man who passes us in the street, for their reality is renewed, as the ordinary mortal's is not, each time those magical verbal symbols pass before the eyes of an imaginative reader or listener. If this creativity be the criterion of great literature, then the German Poetic Realists of the Novelle have added richly to its permanent store.

NOTES

NOTES

NOTES

CHAPTER ONE

1. Franz Stuckert, "Theodor Storms novellistische Form," in *Germanisch-romanische Monatsschrift*, 27 (1939), 24-39.
2. "Nachricht von den poetischen Werken des Johannes Boccaccio," in *Friedrich Schlegels prosaische Jugendschriften*, ed. Minor, 2. Aufl. (Wien: Konegen, 1906), 412-413.
3. Ludwig Tieck's *Schriften* (Berlin: Reimer, 1828ff.), XI, lxxxvif.
4. "Wunderbar" may also be rendered by "miraculous." Strictly speaking, the latter is ruled out of the Novelle, as belonging to the supernatural world of the "Märchen." Tieck himself, in his earlier Novellen, as well as Goethe in *Novelle*, indulges in this "adulteration" of supernaturalism. Strangely enough, Paul Ernst, stressing the element of the improbable, even impossible, in the Novelle, calls it the sister of the fairy-tale (*Der Weg zur Form*, 1928, 288).
5. *Deutscher Novellenschatz* (München: Oldenbourg, [1871]), I, xviiff.
6. *Jugenderinnerungen und Bekenntnisse*, 3. Aufl. (Berlin: Hertz, 1900), 344-345, 348.
7. The context indicates that Heyse had Goethe's *Elective Affinities* in mind here, a work that, though expanded into a novel, remains essentially a Novelle. There is some plausibility in Heyse's suggestion (*Novellenschatz* I, ix-x) that the experimental methods of contemporary science favored the "isolating" form of the Novelle in this period.
8. Heyse does in fact say (xx) that such a simple formula as that of Boccaccio's falcon-story could not be expected to apply to all modern Novellen, but that "it would do no harm" if writers would begin by asking themselves where the "falcon" in their matter is.
9. From a subsequently withdrawn preface of June, 1881; *Sämtl. Werke*, ed. Köster, VIII, 122. Echoed briefly in Storm's letter of August 14, 1881, to Keller; Storm-Keller *Briefwechsel*, ed. Köster, 114.
10. Friedrich Spielhagen, *Beiträge zur Theorie und Technik des Romans* (Leipzig: Staackmann, 1883), 245-246; also *Neue Beiträge zur Theorie und Technik der Epik und Dramatik*, ibid., 1898, 74.
11. Johannes Klein, "Wesen und Erscheinungsformen der deutschen Novelle," in *Germanisch-romanische Monatsschrift*, 24 (1936), 81-100.
12. F. Th. Vischer, *Aesthetik oder Wissenschaft des Schönen* (originally Stuttgart, 1857), 2. Aufl., ed. Robert Vischer (München: Meyer & Jessen, 1922-23), VI, 192-193. Vischer also (193) quotes with approval the definition of the Novelle as one situation vs. the novel as a series of situations.
13. Georg von Lukács, *Die Seele und die Formen. Essays* (Berlin: Fleischel, 1911), 158, thus defines the scope of the Novelle. A somewhat later definition of his is cited at the beginning of Chapter V, below.
14. The "Kurzgeschichte," not nearly so well developed in Germany as with us, often has the character of a newspaper *feuilleton*. The longer "Erzählung," of which Eichendorff's *Aus dem Leben eines Taugenichts*

is a good example, is essentially a reduced novel, lacking the concentration and intensity of the Novelle.
15. F. Th. Vischer, *op. cit.*, 193.
16. Cf. "dass die epische Prosadichtung sich in dieser Weise [i.e., in the Novelle] gegipfelt und gleichsam die Aufgabe des Dramas übernommen hat," etc.; *Sämtl. Werke*, ed Köster, VIII, 122f.
17. A useful historical account of the Novelle is that by E. K. Bennett, *A History of the German Novelle from Goethe to Thomas Mann* (Cambridge, England: The University Press, 1934).
18. Once the name and the theory of the Novelle had developed, of course, a factor of conscious conformity comes in (as "grammars" affect the development of languages). There is also, to coin a phrase in imitation of Paul Ernst's "Eigenbewegung des Stoffes" (a certain matter calling for a certain form), a sort of "Eigenbewegung der Form" which favors the selection of matter germane to the Novelle.—It is significant for the interrelation of Novelle and drama that Hauptmann has dramatized Hartmann's story.
19. C. H. Herford, "Romanticism in the Modern World," in *Essays and Studies of the English Association*, VIII (1922), 120-121.
20. Ludwig's play *Der Erbförster* (first performed in March 1850) is a more consistent example of Poetic Realism than is his story *Zwischen Himmel und Erde* (published 1856). The latter, unfortunately for our present purpose, though distinguished by some of the qualities of a Novelle, has been enlarged—chiefly through over-elaborate psychological analysis—into something between an "Erzählung" and a "Roman."
21. *Otto Ludwigs gesammelte Schriften*, ed. Stern and Schmidt (Leipzig: Grunow, 1891), VI, 10. Subsequent references in the text and Notes are to this edition.
22. *Nachlasschriften Otto Ludwigs*, ed. Moritz Heydrich (Leipzig: Cnobloch, 1871, 1874), I, 98; *Schriften*, V, 262.
23. "Künstlerisch reproduzierte Wirklichkeit; denn der Schein gemeiner Wirklichkeit muss überall gemieden sein." Letter of September 14, 1858, to Julian Schmidt; *Schriften*, VI, 412.
24. "Wirkliche" and "wahre Natur." Schiller's *Sämtl. Werke*, Säkularausgabe, XII, 233. For all his opposition to Schiller, Ludwig operates to some extent with Schillerian categories.
25. Letter of April 11, 1856; *Schriften*, VI, 390.
26. Adolf Frey, *Erinnerungen an Gottfried Keller*, 3. Aufl. (Leipzig: Haessel, 1919), 43.
27. *Sämtl. Werke*, ed. Merker (München: Müller, 1912-1922), VI, 242, xxix, lv. *Briefe*, ed. Vogtherr (Weimar: Böhlau, 1935), I, 226.
28. Cf. Walter Silz, "Nature in the Tales of Otto Ludwig," in *Modern Language Notes*, XLI (1926), 8-13.
29. Wilhelm Raabe, *Werke* (Berlin-Grunewald: Klemm, n.d.), III, 6, 582.
30. Paul Ernst, *Der Weg zur Form* (München: Müller, 1928), 290: "wie talentlos die Wirklichkeit ist."

CHAPTER TWO

1. The date following the title in this and the subsequent chapters indicates the year of first publication of the Novelle under discussion.

2. Pre-Romantic interest in and admiration of the common folk is shown in Goethe's portrayal of the "Frau aus dem Volke" in the poem *Der Wanderer* and in *Werther*, and the "Bauerbursch" in the second version of *Werther*. There is an interesting parallel with English literature here, from the Pre-Romantic Gray's concern with "the short and simple annals of the poor" to Wordsworth's express poeticizing of the common life. In both countries this tendency is one of the sources of Realism, which thus is rooted in the very heart of Romanticism.

3. In the person of the enlightened Burgomaster, the author scoffs at the superstition, but he does nothing to invalidate it as a factor in his plot.

4. This and subsequent page references in the text are to Brentano's *Werke*, ed. Dohmke (Leipzig & Wien: Bibl. Inst., n.d.)

5. Thus he calls to our attention the smoke-blackened and blood-spattered wreath through which Kasper has shot himself and which Anna Margaret is taking to Annerl as his last greeting (109); the rolling and biting head and the blood-spattered clothing of Annerl and Anna Margaret (115); and the head of Annerl, still bleeding and sadly smiling, held aloft by the executioner (121)!—Brentano's preoccupation with blood, both as a religious and a pathological phenomenon, will doubtless some day be made the subject of a dissertation by a sufficiently hardy mind.

6. The telling little detail of his spurred boots showing beneath his elegant dressing-gown (119) is the only touch of realism about him.

7. There is a marked use of ironical ambiguity or "Doppeldeutigkeit" of expression in other passages of the story.

8. From the frequently over-wrought "Ehrbegriff" which came to dominate the officers' code of 19th-century Germany, that of the "schlagende Verbindungen" or duelling fraternities of the German universities is historically derived.

9. Kasper has a literary forbear in Gretchen's brother Valentin, likewise a simple, honorable soldier who does his duty, as he sees it, unflinchingly, and who speaks his own epitaph in his dying words: "Ich gehe durch den Todesschlaf / Zu Gott ein als Soldat und brav" (*Faust*, 3774f.). Kasper is made of finer and more destructible stuff than Valentin, but the quality summed up in "brav," or the more modern "stramm," is common to both men.

10. The "Kindesmörderin" motif, including that of the refusal to incriminate the (higher-class) lover, is a heritage from the "Sturm und Drang."

11. Only of Annerl does the "outer" narrator catch a glimpse at the very end, after her execution.

NOTES

CHAPTER THREE

1. This and subsequent page references in the text are to *Achim von Arnims Werke*, ausgewählt und herausg. von Reinhold Steig (Leipzig: Insel-Verlag, [1911]), vol. I.
2. They were duly listed among the items taken over from the old garrison (268). Arnim is very careful to prepare for such touches; thus the impregnableness of the fort was at once recognized by the delighted Francoeur (268), and the fireworks theme was also "planted" early (261).
3. In connection with him, Arnim makes one minor slip: the old soldier's wooden leg is considerably shortened by burning (261), yet later he gets up unaided to light Rosalie downstairs (266).
4. Her death, curiously enough, is definitely localized—in Prague, a city with which a good deal of demonology is traditionally associated. This and other little touches may be due to the folksong traditions in which Arnim was versed.
5. " . . . einem Volke, das Kühnheit immer mehr als Güte zu achten weiss" (279). The various ways of rendering "Kühnheit" and "Güte" —none of them quite with the German flavor—are a small illustration of the difficulties besetting "literature in translation."—Some doubt, incidentally, is cast on the crowd as an index of national character by the fact that it was represented shortly before as cursing Rosalie and her husband (276).

CHAPTER FOUR

1. In a letter of December 15, 1838, to her friend Schlüter.
2. Textual references are to volume III of Annette's *Sämtliche Werke*, edited by K. S. Kemminghausen and others (München: Müller, 1925).
3. See the present writer's article "Problems of Weltanschauung in the works of A. v. Droste-Hülshoff," in *PMLA*, LXIV (1949), 683f.
4. Only when she likens a person to a hop-pole (Hopfenstange, 28), or speaks of a good wine-year (33f.), does Annette think in terms of her later Bodensee abode instead of her Westphalian homeland.
5. The business of the spoon, which this time Friedrich "cuts clean through" (as he soon will his own life) shows how readily the artistic use of significant objects in Poetic Realism can pass over into symbolism. We shall observe this later in the case of C. F. Meyer.
6. Thus, Margret's puzzling words, "Ein falscher Eid, ein falscher Eid!" (19), are explained by a passage, later excised, in which a gossipy neighbor tells Margret that Simon had sworn a solemn oath in court denying the paternity of his illegitimate son (see *Die Judenbuche. Mit sämtlichen jüngst wiederaufgefundenen Vorarbeiten*, etc., ed. Kemminghausen [Dortmund: Ruhfus, 1925], 154f.). Friedrich's words to Brandes, "Ihr habt gesagt, was Ihr nicht verantworten könnt, *und ich vielleicht auch*" (25; italics mine), make full sense only in the earliest version, where Friedrich has cast aspersions on Brandes'

mother (*ibid.*, 182). On the other hand, the scar that makes possible the positive identification of Friedrich's body (53) is not prepared for, oddly enough, in any of the versions.

7. Annette here anticipates a later conception of tragic guilt which we associate with Hebbel and Ibsen, but which is also approximated by Theodor Storm. Speaking to Alfred Biese, Storm rejected the older view, based on the determination of a "speziell *eigene* Schuld des Helden," as too narrow and juristic; "wir büssen im Leben viel öfter für die Schuld des Allgemeinen, wovon wir ein Teil sind, für die Menschheit des Zeitalters, worin wir leben," etc. See *Briefwechsel zwischen Th. Storm u. G. Keller*, ed. Köster, 3. Aufl. (Berlin: Paetel, 1909), 10f.
8. Cf. a precedent, p. 11; and the attitude of the crowd: "Packt den Juden!" etc., p. 37.
9. Keller's *Sämtliche Werke*, ed. Fränkel, VII, 97. As a study in social deterioration, including a complete picture of specific locale in terms of "Heimatkunst," *Die Judenbuche* is a forerunner of Keller's story. It is interesting to observe, moreover, that the *Judenbuche* is exactly contemporaneous with Immermann's *Oberhof*, and with it launches the modern "Dorfgeschichte"—another respect in which the "isolated" career of Annette parallels that of her age.
10. Under physical torment, Friedrich attempted suicide by drowning in the Bosporus. This is the implication (sometimes misconstrued) of p. 48, where the Baron raises a shocked finger. At the end, it is mental torment that again makes Friedrich seek escape in death.
11. He doubtless intended simply to beat up Aaron and take money from him, in conformity with a "pattern" that had been implanted in his childhood mind (11)—when stronger powers took matters out of his hands.

CHAPTER FIVE

1. Georg Lukács, *Die Theorie des Romans*. Ein geschichtsphilosophischer Versuch über die Formen der Epik (Berlin: Cassirer, 1920), 38.
2. This and subsequent page references in the text are to volume 3 of Stifter's *Sämmtliche Werke* (Prag: Calve, 1911), which is vol. 22 of the *Bibliothek deutscher Schriftsteller aus Böhmen*.
3. Some incidents, too, seem to be echoes of the Old Testament; for example, the father's reception of Abdias on his first homecoming is strongly reminiscent of that of the Prodigal Son.
4. "Wir alle haben eine tigerartige Anlage, wie wir eine himmlische haben, und wenn die tigerartige nicht geweckt wird, so meinen wir, sie sei garnicht da und es herrsche bloss die himmlische." *Erzählungen*, ed. Johannes Aprent (Pest: Heckenast, 1869), II, 260 (in the brief tale *Zuversicht*).
5. Schiller's poem *Shakespeares Schatten*, lines 35-36.
6. In this respect she is resembled by Peter, the younger of the two brothers in Ponten's Novelle *Der Gletscher*.

7. That both fathers prefer to converse with their daughters in Arabic, and build for them strongholds that prove no protection, are further elements in common.
8. Later on there is a similar meditation on the "miraculous event" of gaining sight: such things will remain miraculous only so long as we have not fathomed those vast powers of Nature in which our life floats, and learned to bind or loose the loving bond between these forces and our life (90).
9. "Es gibt nichts Grosses und nichts Kleines. Der Bau des durch Menschenaugen kaum sichtlichen Tierchens ist bewundernswert und unermesslich gross, die einfache Rundung des Sirius ist klein," etc. *Sämmtl. Wke.* (Prag ed.), v. 18, 189 (letter of February 3, 1854, to Friedrich Culemann).
10. Cited by Konrad Steffen, *Adalbert Stifter und der Aufbau seiner Weltanschauung* (Horgen-Zürich: Münster, 1931), 41.

Chapter Six

1. Letter to Gustav Heckenast, Dec. 19, [1847?]. *Sämtliche Werke*, ed. Sauer (Wien: Schroll, [1909ff.]), Abt. III, 3, No. 663.
2. *Ibid.*, Abt. II, 11, No. 3979. Cf. also *Sämtl. Wke.*, ed. Sauer (Stuttgart: Cotta, [1892]), 18, 198: an "anspruchslose Erzählung," not to be compared with a masterwork of Goethe's.
3. Letter to Graf Majláth, Nov. 20, 1846. *Sämtl. Wke.* (Wien), Abt. III, 3, No. 652.
4. See Heyse's letter of June 11, 1871, to Grillparzer. In replying (June 16, 1870) to Heyse's original request to reprint the *Spielmann*, Grillparzer had echoed Heyse's designation "Novelle" seemingly without conviction. *Sämtl. Wke.* (Wien), Abt. III, 5, Nos. 1733, 1736.
5. It is, again, indicative of the kinship of Novelle and drama that Hauptmann converted Grillparzer's story into a play (*Elga*) with little effort or change.
6. This and subsequent page numbers in the text refer to *Sämtl. Wke.* (Wien), Abt. I, 13 (published 1930).
7. Cf. Ernst Alker, "Komposition und Stil von Grillparzers Novelle 'Der arme Spielmann' " in *Neophilologus*, v. 11 (1925-26), 21.
8. There are striking similarities between Brentano's story and Grillparzer's: 1) the general situation: a higher-class interlocutor elicits a life-story from a simple old person (Anna Margaret and Jakob have a number of traits in common, and a like effect on the interlocutor); 2) the professional opinions of the interlocutor-author that are interjected; 3) the "analytic" procedure; 4) the double frame, with the "outer" narrator participating in the action and the "inner" narrator dying in the course of it, in both stories.
9. Thus we see the narrator both through his self-characterization and through his effect on Jakob, Jakob's landlady, and Barbara. We see Barbara through the fond eyes of her lover and, at the end, the unprejudiced eyes of the narrator: an un-retouched, real-life portrait of a

stout woman, past middle age, inappropriately dressed, "bossy" and tactless, who, it seems, could not ever have been good-looking (80).
10. See F. C. Prescott, *The Poetic Mind* (New York: Macmillan, 1922), 184ff.
11. *Sämtl. Wke.* (Wien), Abt. I, 16, 98-99.
12. *Ibid.*, Abt. I, 7, 22.
13. Letter of Aug. 31, 1806. *Werke*, ed. Minde-Pouet (Leipzig: Bibl. Inst., [1937]), II, 152.
14. Keller's letter to Emil Kuh, Sept. 10, 1871.
15. It is interesting, and consistent with the *epic* attitude maintained by Grillparzer in this story, that he does not insert the song verbatim as a "lyrische Einlage" and "Stimmungsmittel" such as the Romantic narrators who followed Goethe were fond of, and such as Storm, for example, still operates with in *In Sankt Jürgen*.
16. Very like this in effect is Storm's last echoing of the motif of the water-lily at the end of *Immensee*.

CHAPTER SEVEN

1. Keller's *Sämtliche Werke*, ed. Fränkel (Erlenbach-Zürich-München: Rentsch, 1926ff.), VII, 182. All subsequent references to the text of *Romeo und Julia* are to pages of this volume.
2. In contrast to Meyer, whose individual "frames" are sometimes extremely elaborate, Keller develops the cyclical frame, which he brings to supreme mastery in *Das Sinngedicht*. See Priscilla M. Kramer, *The Cyclical Method of Composition in Gottfried Keller's "Sinngedicht,"* New York, 1939 (Ottendorfer Germanic Monographs, No. 26).

CHAPTER EIGHT

1. Adolf Frey, *Conrad Ferdinand Meyer. Sein Leben und seine Werke.* 3. Aufl. (Stuttgart: Cotta, 1919), 288-289.
2. *Briefe Conrad Ferdinand Meyers*, ed. Adolf Frey (Leipzig: Haessel, 1908), II, 510. Henceforward cited as *"Bfe."*
3. Letter of April 19, 1880: " . . . des rein aus meinem Gemüte gehobenen und in der Wirklichkeit schwer ein Analogon findenden Charakters des Heiligen" (*Bfe.* II, 347).
4. See his letter to Spitteler, *Bfe.* I, 426-427.
5. Letter to Betty Paoli, April 9, 1884, *Bfe.* II, 349.
6. See Meyer's own remarks on his methods of work, quoted by Adolf Frey, *C. F. Meyer*, 1919, 288.
7. One could make such a summary out of Canon Burkhard's words in the opening "frame" which would run about like this: "Wahre Geschichte von einem Heiligen, der seinem König, dessen treuer Diener und ärgster Feind er war, Leib und Seele zerstörte und ihm selbst zum Opfer fiel." See Meyer's *Werke*, Neue Oktav-Ausgabe (Leipzig: Haessel, 1926), IV, 16. All page references for *Der Heilige* are to this volume.

8. See Chapter One, above, p. 3.
9. See Otto Ludwig's words, Chapter One, above, p. 12.
10. This is not always managed with complete plausibility; for example, his detailed observation of Becket's face (even to the "Staatsfalte" between the eyes) from ambush (67). Occasionally, too, Hans's language is too poetic or learned for his "character."
11. The device of "framing" is so habitual with Meyer that he frames even an interpolated episode such as that which relates Hans's use of a Moorish phrase to Becket (46f.). The author introduces it indeed with a Boccaccian superscription, "How Hans and Thomas laid their fingers on their lips," and rounds off his little anecdote with this gesture, used at beginning and end in two different senses.
12. It is characteristic of Meyer that a trait like Hans's Swiss thrift, subtly noted at the end of the first chapter (10), is carried through to the end, where we are told of his cannily marrying a propertied widow and setting himself up in business ere his fame should fade (201f.).
13. There seems to be a reminiscence here (84, 85), both in situation and words, of Uhland's ballad *Die Rache*.
14. See the writer's essay "Otto Ludwig and the Process of Poetic Creation," in *PMLA*, LX (1945), especially pp. 868ff.
15. August Langmesser, *C. F. Meyer. Sein Leben, seine Werke und sein Nachlass*. 3. Aufl. (Berlin: Wiegandt & Grieben, 1905), 314. The passage (cited also by Robert Faesi, *C. F. Meyer*, 2. Aufl., 1948, 131) is in a letter which has not been accessible to me.
16. Letter of April 21, 1881. *Louise von François und Conrad Ferdinand Meyer. Ein Briefwechsel*, ed. Anton Bettelheim, 2. verm. Aufl. (Berlin and Leipzig: De Gruyter, 1920), 2. Cited hereafter as "François-Meyer *Bfw*."
17. It may be considered typical of the Victorian age in contrast to the modern, that whereas in Tennyson's play *Becket* (1884) the hero's motivation is simple (worldly ambition and desire for power), T. S. Eliot's Thomas, in *Murder in the Cathedral* (1935), remains enigmatical, like Meyer's: does he desire martyrdom, or merely foresee it? Is he in truth free of all the worldly and "professional" ambitions suggested by the Four Tempters (objectivations of his mind)? His valedictory Christmas Sermon itself is not simple.
18. They both, however, pray the Lord's Prayer (77). There is, incidentally, a suggestion of the relations of Lessing's Nathan and Recha in this pair.
19. See Carol K. Bang, *Maske und Gesicht in den Werken C. F. Meyers* (Baltimore: Johns Hopkins Press, 1940), 89f.
20. Letter of Carsamstag, 1882; François-Meyer *Bfw.*, 48. There is doubtless an element of unconscious self-deception in this disparagement of his lyrics; see Emil Staiger in *Weltliteratur. Festgabe für Strich* (Bern: Francke, 1952), 117.
21. Adolf Frey, *C. F. Meyer*, 1919, 309, 298.

22. Hans's own diction seems embellished through the influence of this example, as Meyer remarks with characteristic self-irony (49).
23. A subtly characterizing gesture is Becket's smoothing Richard's hair with gentle, *motherly* hand (161).
24. This startling change of attitude is pointed up by King Henry's involuntarily comical indignation at the idea: "So spricht kein Bischof," etc., 135f.
25. Gnade is, like Recha, an unplausible mixture of childlikeness and "Altklugheit." "Du darfst nicht an den Hof, in diesen Pesthauch, wo nichts Reines gedeiht" (79) sounds like Odoardo.
26. Betsy Meyer, *Conrad Ferdinand Meyer in der Erinnerung seiner Schwester* (Berlin: Paetel, 1903), 161, 176f.
27. Thomas Mann, *Unordnung und frühes Leid.* Novelle (Berlin: S. Fischer, [1926]), 36.
28. Adolf Frey, *C. F. Meyer*, 1919, 307.
29. Letter of late May, 1881; François-Meyer *Bfw.*, 12. Meyer's attitude is not inconsonant with that of Otto Ludwig, who begins a discussion *Der poetische Realismus* with the sentence "Das Dargestellte soll nicht gemeine Wirklichkeit sein," etc. (V, 264). It is, after all, a question of degree of nearness to Naturalism.
30. Adolf Frey, *C. F. Meyer*, 1919, 307.
31. François-Meyer *Bfw.*, 176.

CHAPTER NINE

1. *Theodor Storms sämtliche Werke in acht Bänden*, ed. Albert Köster (Leipzig: Insel-Verlag, 1923), VII, 311. All subsequent references to Storm's works, unless otherwise noted, are to this edition—for the *Schimmelreiter*, to vol. VII of it by pages.
2. *Am Kamin*, II, 163. "Einsamkeit" of landscape and individual is one of the themes that repeat in the *Schimmelreiter*; cf., of numerous instances, 261, 264, 346, 350, 352.
3. Of Storm's Novellen, especially *Carsten Curator* and *John Riew'* represent the inexorable power of heredity as a form of fate. The case of his own ill-starred son led Storm to brood over a *culpa patris*: see *Briefwechsel zwischen Paul Heyse und Theodor Storm*, ed. G. J. Plotke (München: Lehmann, 1917-18), I, 177f.
4. *Briefwechsel zwischen Theodor Storm und Gottfried Keller*, ed. Köster, 3. Aufl. (Berlin: Paetel, 1909), 10f. Cf. also Gertrud Storm, *Theodor Storm* (1913), II, 175f.
5. The father-son solidarity, most poignantly expressed in the deathbed scene (294f.) is the converse of the father-son conflicts which are one of Storm's obsessing themes (e.g., *Carsten Curator, Eekenhof, Der Herr Etatsrat, Hans und Heinz Kirch*). Hauke, as the man of superior mind who collides with the inert and superstitious crowd, is the continuation of his father, "der klügste Mann im Dorf" (282, 299), and of his grandfather, another prodigy who mastered Euclid and Dutch (258). The son's intolerance of human stupidity and sloth

is found already in the father (Tede's tirade on the Deichgraf, 270, and his mockery, 274), and Hauke's opponents extend their enmity to his father (279). To Storm, with his strong "Sippengefühl," these generational continuities were doubtless important, and the fact that two families, one declining, the other "coming up," terminate in a feeble-minded girl, must have been for him a real part of the tragedy. It is characteristic of Storm that he should, in the opening paragraph, link with the narrator his ancient great-grandmother (actually Storm's own), and later emphasize such symbols as the antique "Wandbett," in which generations have slept and died (303) and which the innovator Hauke dispenses with (313).

6. On Storm's attitude toward death and immortality, see the writer's article in *PMLA*, LXI (1946), 767-769.
7. Letter of March 12, 1888, quoted by Hans Eichentopf, *Theodor Storms Erzählungskunst* (Marburg: Elwert, 1908), 27.
8. *Heyse-Storm Briefwechsel*, II, 170, 198.
9. See Storm's *Werke*, ed. Theo. Hertel and others (Leipzig: Bibl. Inst., [1936]), VIII, 398f. Just as one-sided, on the other hand, is the judgment of Willy Seidel, *Die Natur als Darstellungsmittel in den Erzählungen Theo. Storms* (München: Oldenbourg, 1911), 17, that the entire action of the *Schimmelreiter* consists in a battle of man against Nature.
10. Later on, two men who have been out on watch (255) and therefore have not heard the discussion, independently report the same observation (297). They, to be sure, may be thought to be familiar with the local legend; but not so the Traveller.
11. The coarse horse-trader standing "sperrbeinig" on the road has a little similarity to the Abdecker von Döbbeln in Kleist's story; also the remarkable restoration of the Schimmel reminds one of that of Kohlhaas's "Rappen." There is perhaps also a reminiscence of the miraculous way in which Bertrand comes by Johanna's helmet, and Schiller's "braun Bohemerweib" is a sister to Storm's swarthy Slovak.
12. In the latter respect, *Der Schimmelreiter* differs greatly from Ludwig's *Zwischen Himmel und Erde*, which it resembles in the use of individual dramatic scenes, technical details of "Beruf" (slate-roofing and dike-building), and repetitive leitmotifs.
13. The use of colors, while not so striking as that of sounds, is noteworthy. See the writer's article in *PMLA*, LXI (1946), 774f.
14. Alliterations are frequent, especially on consonants but also on vowels. For examples, see *PMLA*, LXI (1946), 776.
15. The gesture of a very old woman stroking the head of a child is repeated: 252, 355. It is interesting to observe how Storm uses such simple "business" over again, e.g., that of a man leaning in a doorway (273, 290, 331, 354), or a man deliberately "stowing his quid" (260, 343).
16. More than a score of instances of each could be cited. Their themes, of course, are frequently connected with that of the ocean. At one

point, where it blinds Hauke to the extent of the damage to the dike, the sunlight has a decisive influence on the action (360).
17. The lark-motif, on the other hand, is concomitant with smiling summer skies: 339, 353, 360; once, however, it is used to point up Nature's rapacity: 325.
18. With the light-motif is combined a verbal motif of security: Hauke feels reassured about wife and child, for "auf unsre Werfte steigt das Wasser nicht" (369); again, "sein Weib, sein Kind, sie sassen sicher auf der hohen Werfte" (370); "Weib und Kind, gottlob, sie sassen sicher auf der hohen Werfte" (373); "der Lichtschein . . . noch immer brannte der auf seiner Werfte" (374); "noch immer ragte die Werfte . . . aus dem Schwall hervor, noch immer schimmerte von dort der Lichtschein" (375).
19. The mothers, curiously enough, are omitted altogether, as they are in *Der arme Spielmann* and *Der Heilige*—perhaps a mark of the economy of the Novelle in contrast to the novel.
20. Storm shows a pronounced fondness for such symbolic objects as the Esche. Another one is the "Lehnstuhl," the curule chair of Elke's father, with whom it is associated through several mentions (272, 276, 296, 297). It is no mere chance that Hauke is first shown sitting down in it on the occasion when he broaches to Elke the great new project which is to prove that he deserves his office; and now he grips both its arms with characteristic tenacity (312). Later, after winning his fight in the council, he sits down again in the armchair of his predecessor (330). Still later, distraught with cares concerning his dike, he throws himself into the armchair but immediately quits it again, as though he felt uncertain of his tenancy (358).

Chapter Ten

1. Gerhart Hauptmann, *Gesammelte Werke* in acht Bänden (Berlin: Fischer, 1921), V, 37-39. All subsequent references in the text are to pages of this volume.
2. Hauptmann uses irony elsewhere in the story, e.g., in the fact that Thiel, who has always been so scrupulous about lowering his gates (though hardly anyone ever passed over that remote crossing), must see his own child run over by a train; or that Lene, just before her death, is deeply changed for the better, yet the new woman, so to speak, is killed for the misdeeds of the old.
3. It is a "modern" feature of Hauptmann's story that he uses actual place-names of the vicinity of Berlin instead of the invented places of older fiction.
4. But Minna, too, is not idealized nor made especially attractive. Hauptmann gives the briefest, soberest "life" of her: she appears one Sunday with Thiel in church; another Sunday marries him, and shares his pew and hymn-book for two years, her delicate face a contrast to his; then one weekday the bell tolls for her, and the next Sunday Thiel is again alone in his pew (11).

5. Büchner's fragmentary narrative *Lenz* (1836) is a marvellous study in mental deterioration, far in advance of its times. Had it been completed, it would probably have been one of the great psychological Novellen of the century.
6. Grillparzer's *Sämtliche Werke*, Wien edition, Abt. I, vol. 13, p. 79.
7. *Promethidenlos* (1885) does not really count, as it was recalled after publication.
8. Georg von Lukács, *Die Seele und die Formen*, 165.

Index of Names

A.

Alker, Ernst, 160.
Arnim, L. Achim v., 11, 14, 17, 29-35, 156.
Auerbach, Berthold, 14.

B.

Bang, Carol K., 162.
Beethoven, Ludwig van, 54.
Bennett, Edwin K., 156.
Bismarck, Otto v., 151.
Blake, William, 60.
Boccaccio, Giovanni di, 1, 2, 3, 4, 7, 9, 155.
Brentano, Clemens M., 8, 11, 14, 17-28, 33, 35, 64, 70, 72, 75, 78, 139, 146, 151, 157, 160.
Büchner, Georg, 36, 146, 166.
Byron, Lord, 59.

C.

Cervantes, Miguel de, 1, 67.
Chamisso, Adelbert v., 18, 36, 72.
Chaucer, Geoffrey, 1, 36.
Coleridge, S. T., 22.

D.

Droste-Hülshoff, Annette v., 18, 36-51, 68, 72, 81, 125, 158f.

E.

Eckermann, J. P., 2.
Eckhart, Meister, 24.
Eichendorff, Joseph v., 18, 144, 155f.
Eliot, T. S., 162.
Ernst, Paul, 3, 15, 153, 156.

F.

Feuerbach, Ludwig, 11.
François, Louise v., 102, 105, 109.
Frey, Adolf, 94, 105, 109, 162.

G.

Goethe, Johann Wolfgang v., 1, 2, 3, 5, 6, 7, 8, 10, 11, 25, 27, 29, 34, 36, 38, 48, 50, 56, 59, 60, 66, 67, 72, 73, 143, 155, 157.
Gray, Thomas, 157.
Grillparzer, Franz, 18, 27, 55, 60, 67-78, 108, 149, 150, 160f., 166.
Grimm Brothers (Jakob and Wilhelm), 18, 36.
Grolman, Adolf v., 3.

H.

Haessel, Hermann, 105.
Hardy, Thomas, 25.
Hartmann von Aue, 10, 34.
Hauptmann, Gerhart, 8, 28, 107, 137-151, 160, 165f.
Hebbel, Friedrich, 14, 55, 89, 118, 159.
Hegel, G. W. F., 48.
Heine, Heinrich, 18, 72.
Herford, C. H., 12, 156.
Heyse, Paul, 4, 5, 6, 9, 17, 30, 37, 67, 80, 84, 97, 138, 155, 160.
Hildebrandslied, 24.
Hoffmann, E. T. A., 8, 39, 62, 89.

I.

Ibsen, Henrik, 14, 159.

K.

Kafka, Franz, 13.
Kant, Immanuel, 11.
Karl Eugen, Duke of Württemberg, 22.
Keller, Gottfried, 8, 14, 15, 47, 49, 63, 75, 76, 79-93, 96, 107, 108, 109, 151, 155, 156, 159, 161.
Kerner, Justinus, 143.
Klein, Johannes, 6, 155.
Kleist, Heinrich v., 1, 2, 6, 7, 8, 12, 18, 19, 25, 31, 34, 35, 38, 44, 47, 67, 69, 70, 73, 74, 80, 120, 121, 124, 126, 138, 162.
Köster, Albert, 128, 155.
Kramer, Priscilla M., 161.
Kurz, Hermann, 4, 9.

L.

Langmesser, August, 162.
Lenau, Nikolaus, 59.
Lingg, Hermann, 96, 101.
Ludwig, Otto, 8, 12, 13, 14, 15, 23, 41, 55, 61, 119, 143, 144, 156, 163, 164.
Lukács, Georg (v.), 52, 155, 159, 166.

M.

Mann, Thomas, 9, 20, 21, 23, 68, 74, 108, 163.
Margaret of Navarre, 1.
Meyer, Conrad Ferdinand, 8, 9, 43, 57, 68, 73, 79, 94-116, 121, 151, 161ff.
Mörike, Eduard, 36, 68.

N.

Napoleon Bonaparte, 11, 59.
Nibelungenlied, 112.
Nicolai, C. F., 3.
Novalis (Friedrich v. Hardenberg), 78, 82.

P.

Paoli, Betty, 94.
Poe, Edgar Allan, 72.
Ponten, Josef, 159.
Prescott, F. C., 161.

R.

Raabe, Wilhelm, 15, 121, 156.
Riehl, W. H., 32.

S.

Schelling, F. W., 11.
Schiller, J. Friedrich v., 12, 13, 16, 46, 48, 56, 71, 79, 88, 89, 92, 94, 118, 156, 159, 164.
Schlegel, August Wilhelm (v.), 3.
Schlegel, Friedrich (v.), 3, 69, 97, 155.
Schmidt, Erich, 6.
Schnitzler, Arthur, 24.
Schopenhauer, Arthur, 11, 59.
Scott, Walter, 9.
Shakespeare, William, 8, 80, 88, 92-93.
Spielhagen, Friedrich, 5, 155.

Staiger, Emil, 162.
Stifter, Adalbert, 37, 52-66, 159f.
Storm, Theodor, 5, 6, 8, 14, 37, 68, 70, 117-136, 140, 145, 150, 151, 155, 159, 161, 163ff.
Strauss, David Friedrich, 11.
Stuckert, Franz, 155.
Sudermann, Hermann, 153.

T.

Tennyson, Alfred Lord, 162.
Thierry, Augustin, 94, 96.
Tieck, J. Ludwig, 3, 4, 5, 11, 17, 18, 30, 37, 40, 78, 144, 155.

U.

Uhland, Ludwig, 162.

V.

Viebig, Clara, 34.
Vischer, Friedrich Theodor, 6, 7, 155, 156.
Voss, Johann Heinrich, 60.

W.

Wagner, Richard, 34, 82.
Walther von der Vogelweide, 61.
Wedekind, Frank, 149.
Wieland, Christoph Martin, 1, 2.
William II, German Emperor, 151.
Wordsworth, William, 157.

www.ingramcontent.com/pod-product-compliance
Lightning Source LLC
Chambersburg PA
CBHW031314150426
43191CB00005B/224